The Essential Air Fryer Cookbook for UK Kitchens

Quick, Easy, and Nutritious Recipes for Everyday Meals

Tammy B. Lockett

Notice Of Disclaimer.

Please note that the information in this document is intended for educational and entertainment purposes only. Every effort has been made to provide accurate, up-to-date, reliable and complete information. No warranty of any kind is declared or implied. The reader acknowledges that the author does not engage in the provision of legal, financial, medical or professional advice. The content in this book has been obtained from a variety of sources. Please consult a licensed professional before attempting any of the techniques described in this book. By reading this document, the reader agrees that in no event shall the author be liable for any direct or indirect damages, including but not limited to errors, omissions or inaccuracies, resulting from the use of the information in this document.

Table of Content

Beef, Pork & Lamb Recipes 37

Fish And Seafood Recipes 46

Vegetarian Recipes 55

Vegetable Side Dishes Recipes 64

Sandwiches And Burgers Recipes 72

INTRODUCTION

Still crave for the deep-fried food that is not healthy?

Tired of the fuss of preparing and cooking food in busy weeknights?

Want to create healthy food without sacrificing the taste?

Are you ready to revolutionize your cooking experience and savor the benefits of healthier, more flavorful meals? Look no further than this comprehensive guide to air frying excellence!

This cookbook is meticulously crafted to cater to both novice and experienced home cooks, offering a wide array of recipes that go beyond the ordinary. From crispy appetizers to succulent main courses and indulgent desserts, you'll discover a world of exciting flavors and textures that showcase the true potential of your air fryer.

Elevate Your Culinary Game:

Discover the secrets to creating crispy, golden perfection with minimal oil and maximum taste. From succulent meats to vibrant veggies and indulgent desserts, this cookbook will transform the way you perceive home cooking.

Budget-Friendly and Time-Saving:

Embrace the convenience of air frying and save money on takeaways without compromising on flavor. With ingredients easily found at your local grocery store and quick cooking times, you'll wonder how you ever managed without this incredible appliance.

Beginner-Friendly Guidance:

Whether you're an air frying novice or a seasoned pro, our clear, step-by-step instructions ensure success with every recipe. Gain confidence in the kitchen and impress your loved ones with stunning, restaurant-quality dishes.

Inside this game-changing cookbook, you'll find:

Healthy and nutritious breakfast

Juicy Beef, Pork, and Lamb Recipes

Healthy vegetable meals and side dishes

Mouth-watering Fish and Seafood Recipes

Flavorsome Vegan & Vegetable Recipes

Extra delicious no-fuss desserts and snacks

And so much more…

"The Essential Air Fryer Cookbook for UK Kitchens" is more than just a collection of recipes; it's your passport to a world of culinary delights. Perfect for busy professionals, health-conscious individuals, and foodies alike, this book will become your go-to resource for creating memorable, mouthwatering meals.

Don't wait another minute to transform your kitchen and your life! Click "Buy Now" and embark on a flavorful adventure with the power of air frying at your fingertips. Your taste buds will thank you!

Bread And Breakfast

Lorraine Egg Cups

Servings: 6
Prep Time: 10 Minutes | Cooking Time: 30 Minutes
Ingredients:

- 3 eggs
- 2 tbsp half-and-half
- Garlic salt and pepper to taste
- 2 tbsp diced white onion
- 1 tbsp dried parsley
- 85g cooked bacon, crumbled
- 1/4 cup grated Swiss cheese
- 1 tomato, sliced

Directions:

1. Preheat air fryer at 175°C/350°F.
2. Whisk the egg, half-and-half, garlic sea salt, parsley and black pepper in a bowl.
3. Divide onion, bacon, and cheese between 6 lightly greased silicone cupcakes. Spread the egg mixture between cupcakes evenly. Top each cup with 1 tomato slice.
4. Place them in the frying basket and Bake for 8-10 minutes.
5. Serve immediately.
6. **Variations & Ingredients Tips:**
7. Add some chopped spinach or kale for extra veggies.
8. Use smoked salmon or ham instead of bacon.
9. Top with sliced avocado or a dollop of sour cream.
10. **Per serving:** Calories: 140; Total Fat: 10g; Saturated Fat: 4g; Cholesterol: 130mg; Sodium: 310mg; Total Carbs: 2g; Dietary Fiber: 0g; Total Sugars: 1g; Protein: 10g

Breakfast Sausage Bites

Servings: 4
Prep Time: 10 Minutes | Cooking Time: 30 Minutes
Ingredients:

- 454g ground pork sausages
- 1/4 cup diced onions
- 1 tsp rubbed sage
- 1/4 tsp ground nutmeg
- 1/2 tsp fennel seeds
- 1/4 tsp garlic powder
- 2 tbsp parsley, chopped
- Salt and pepper to taste

Directions:

1. Preheat air fryer at 177°C/350°F.
2. Combine all ingredients except parsley in a bowl.
3. Form mixture into balls.
4. Place balls in a greased air fryer basket.
5. Air fry for 10 minutes, flipping once halfway.
6. Sprinkle with parsley and serve immediately.
7. **Variations & Ingredients Tips:**
8. Use turkey or chicken sausage for less fat.
9. Add shredded cheese or diced peppers to the mixture.
10. Serve with maple syrup or honey mustard for dipping.
11. **Per Serving:** Calories: 400; Total Fat: 32g; Saturated Fat: 12g; Cholesterol: 80mg; Sodium: 630mg; Total Carbs: 4g; Dietary Fiber: 1g; Total Sugars: 1g; Protein: 21g

Bacon, Broccoli And Swiss Cheese Bread Pudding

Servings: 2
Prep Time: 15 Mins | Cooking Time: 48 Minutes
Ingredients:

- 227g thick cut bacon, cut into 0.6cm pieces
- 3 cups brioche bread or rolls, cut into 1.25cm cubes
- 3 eggs
- 1 cup milk
- 1/2 teaspoon salt
- Freshly ground black pepper
- 1 cup frozen broccoli florets, thawed and chopped
- 1½ cups grated Swiss cheese

Directions:

1. Preheat the air fryer to 205°C/400°F.
2. Air-fry the bacon for 6 minutes until crispy, shaking basket occasionally. Remove bacon to paper towel.
3. Air-fry the brioche cubes for 2 minutes to lightly toast. (Omit if bread is stale.)

4. Butter a 15-18cm cake pan. Combine all ingredients in a bowl and toss well. Transfer to buttered pan, cover with foil and refrigerate overnight or 8 hours.

5. Remove from fridge 1 hour before cooking to come to room temperature.

6. Preheat air fryer to 165°C/330°F. Transfer pan to air fryer basket using a foil sling. Air-fry covered for 20 minutes.

7. Remove foil and air-fry 20 more minutes until custard is set. Cover again if browning too quickly.

8. **Variations & Ingredients Tips**:

9. Use ham or sausage instead of bacon.

10. Add sautéed onions or bell peppers.

11. Substitute cheddar or gruyere for the swiss.

12. **Per Serving**: Calories: 910; Total Fat: 53g; Saturated Fat: 24g; Cholesterol: 360mg; Sodium: 1615mg; Total Carbs: 52g; Dietary Fiber: 3g; Total Sugars: 7g; Protein: 51g

Mediterranean Granola

Servings: 6
Prep Time: 10 Minutes | Cooking Time: 40 Minutes
Ingredients:

- 1 cup rolled oats
- 1/4 cup dried cherries, diced
- 1/4 cup almond slivers
- 1/4 cup hazelnuts, chopped
- 1/4 cup pepitas
- 1/4 cup hemp hearts
- 3 tbsp honey
- 1 tbsp olive oil
- 1 tsp ground cinnamon
- 1/4 tsp ground nutmeg
- 1/4 tsp salt
- 2 tbsp dark chocolate chips
- 3 cups Greek yogurt

Directions:

1. Preheat air fryer to 130°C/260°F.

2. Stir the oats, cherries, almonds, hazelnuts, pepitas, hemp hearts, 2 tbsp of honey, olive oil, cinnamon, nutmeg, and salt in a bowl, mixing well.

3. Pour the mixture onto the parchment-lined frying basket and spread it into a single layer. Bake for 25-30 minutes, shaking twice.

4. Let the granola cool completely. Stir in the chocolate chips.

5. Divide between 6 cups. Top with Greek yogurt and remaining honey to serve.

6. **Variations & Ingredients Tips**:

7. Use dried apricots, figs or dates instead of cherries.

8. Add some chia seeds or flax meal for extra nutrition.

9. Serve with milk, almond milk or coconut yogurt.

10. **Per serving**: Calories: 370; Total Fat: 18g; Saturated Fat: 4g; Cholesterol: 5mg; Sodium: 105mg; Total Carbs: 43g; Dietary Fiber: 6g; Total Sugars: 21g; Protein: 15g

Maple-peach And Apple Oatmeal

Servings: 4
Prep Time: 10 Minutes | Cooking Time: 15 Minutes
Ingredients:

- 2 cups old-fashioned rolled oats
- 1/2 tsp baking powder
- 1 1/2 tsp ground cinnamon
- 1/4 tsp ground flaxseeds
- 1/8 tsp salt
- 1 1/4 cups vanilla almond milk
- 1/4 cup maple syrup
- 1 tsp vanilla extract
- 1 peeled peach, diced
- 1 peeled apple, diced

Directions:

1. Preheat air fryer to 175°C/350°F.

2. Mix oats, baking powder, cinnamon, flaxseed, and salt in a large bowl. Next, stir in almond milk, maple syrup, vanilla, and 3/4 of the diced peaches, and 3/4 of the diced apple.

3. Grease 6 ramekins. Divide the batter evenly between the ramekins and transfer the ramekins to the frying basket.

4. Bake in the air fryer for 8-10 minutes until the top is golden and set.

5. Garnish with the rest of the peaches and apples. Serve.

6. **Variations & Ingredients Tips**:

7. Substitute peaches and apples with berries or bananas.

8. Add some chopped nuts or seeds for crunch.

9. Drizzle with honey or nut butter before serving.

10. **Per serving**: Calories: 320; Total Fat: 6g; Saturated Fat: 0.5g; Cholesterol: 0mg; Sodium: 150mg; Total Carbs: 62g; Dietary Fiber: 7g; Total Sugars: 26g; Protein: 7g

Parsley Egg Scramble With Cottage Cheese

Servings: 2
Prep Time: 5 Minutes | Cooking Time: 15 Minutes
Ingredients:
- 1 tbsp cottage cheese, crumbled
- 4 eggs
- Salt and pepper to taste
- 2 tsp heavy cream
- 1 tbsp chopped parsley

Directions:
1. Preheat air fryer to 200°C/400°F. Grease a baking pan with olive oil.
2. Beat the eggs, salt, and pepper in a bowl. Pour into the pan, place in air fryer basket, and air fry for 5 minutes.
3. Using a spatula, stir in heavy cream, cottage cheese, and half the parsley. Air fry 2 more minutes.
4. Scatter with remaining parsley to serve.
5. **Variations & Ingredients Tips**:
6. Add diced veggies like spinach, tomatoes or peppers.
7. Use milk or plant-based milk instead of cream.
8. Top with shredded cheese or hot sauce.
9. **Per serving**: Calories: 189; Total Fat: 12g; Saturated Fat: 5g; Cholesterol: 429mg; Sodium: 310mg; Total Carbohydrates: 2g; Dietary Fiber: 0g; Total Sugars: 1g; Protein: 17g

Green Strata

Servings: 4
Prep Time: 10 Minutes | Cooking Time: 35 Minutes
Ingredients:
- 5 asparagus, chopped
- 4 eggs
- 3 tablespoons milk
- 1 cup baby spinach, torn
- 2 bread slices, cubed
- ½ cup grated Gruyere cheese
- 2 tablespoons chopped parsley

- Salt and pepper to taste

Directions:
1. Preheat air fryer to 170°C/340°F. Add asparagus spears and 1 tbsp water in a baking pan. Place the pan into the air fryer. Bake until crisp and tender, 3-5 minutes. Remove. Wipe to basket clean and spray with cooking spray. Return asparagus to the pan and arrange the bread cubes.
2. Beat the eggs and milk in a bowl. Then mix in baby spinach and Gruyere cheese, parsley, salt, and pepper. Pour over the asparagus and bread. Return to the fryer and Bake until eggs are set, and the tops browned, 12-14 minutes. Serve warm.
3. **Variations & Ingredients Tips**:
4. Use broccoli, kale or Swiss chard instead of spinach for different greens.
5. Swap Gruyere for cheddar, Swiss or mozzarella cheese.
6. Add some cooked bacon, ham or sausage for a meaty version.
7. **Per Serving**: Calories: 202; Total Fat: 12g; Saturated Fat: 6g; Cholesterol: 205mg; Sodium: 288mg; Total Carbs: 9g; Dietary Fiber: 1g; Total Sugars: 2g; Protein: 15g

Walnut Pancake

Servings: 4
Prep Time: 10 Minutes | Cooking Time: 20 Minutes
Ingredients:
- 3 tablespoons butter, divided into thirds
- 1 cup flour
- 1½ teaspoons baking powder
- ¼ teaspoon salt
- 2 tablespoons sugar
- ¾ cup milk
- 1 egg, beaten
- 1 teaspoon pure vanilla extract
- ½ cup walnuts, roughly chopped
- maple syrup or fresh sliced fruit, for serving

Directions:
1. Place 1 tablespoon of the butter in air fryer baking pan. Cook at 165°C/330°F for 3 minutes to melt.
2. In a small dish or pan, melt the remaining 2 tablespoons of butter either in the microwave or on the stove.

3. In a medium bowl, stir together the flour, baking powder, salt, and sugar. Add milk, beaten egg, the 2 tablespoons of melted butter, and vanilla. Stir until combined but do not beat. Batter may be slightly lumpy.

4. Pour batter over the melted butter in air fryer baking pan. Sprinkle nuts evenly over top.

5. Cook for 20minutes or until toothpick inserted in center comes out clean. Turn air fryer off, close the machine, and let pancake rest for 2minutes.

6. Remove pancake from pan, slice, and serve with syrup or fresh fruit.

7. **Variations & Ingredients Tips**:

8. Substitute different nuts like pecans or almonds for the walnuts.

9. Add chocolate chips, berries or banana slices to the batter.

10. Top with powdered sugar or whipped cream instead of syrup.

11. **Per Serving**: Calories: 300; Total Fat: 17g; Saturated Fat: 6g; Cholesterol: 60mg; Sodium: 290mg; Total Carbs: 32g; Dietary Fiber: 2g; Total Sugars: 8g; Protein: 7g

Carrot Orange Muffins

Servings: 12
Prep Time: 15 Minutes | Cooking Time: 12 Minutes
Ingredients:

- 1½ cups all-purpose flour
- ½ cup granulated sugar
- ½ teaspoon ground cinnamon
- 2 teaspoons baking powder
- ¼ teaspoon baking soda
- ½ teaspoon salt
- 2 large eggs
- ¼ cup vegetable oil
- ⅓ cup orange marmalade
- 2 cups grated carrots

Directions:

1. Preheat the air fryer to 160°C/320°F.

2. In a large bowl, whisk together the flour, sugar, cinnamon, baking powder, baking soda, and salt; set aside.

3. In a separate bowl, whisk together the eggs, vegetable oil, orange marmalade, and grated carrots.

4. Make a well in the dry ingredients; then pour the wet ingredients into the well. Using a rubber spatula, mix for 1 minute or until slightly lumpy.

5. Using silicone muffin liners, fill 6 liners two-thirds full.

6. Carefully place the liners in the air fryer basket and bake for 12 minutes or until tops are browned and a toothpick inserted in center comes out clean.

7. Carefully remove and repeat with remaining batter.

8. Serve warm.

9. **Variations & Ingredients Tips**:

10. Substitute applesauce for some of the oil.

11. Add chopped walnuts or raisins to the batter.

12. Make an orange glaze to drizzle over cooled muffins.

13. **Per Serving**: Calories: 165; Total Fat: 6g; Saturated Fat: 1g; Cholesterol: 35mg; Sodium: 175mg; Total Carbs: 25g; Dietary Fiber: 1g; Total Sugars: 12g; Protein: 3g

Parma Ham & Egg Toast Cups

Servings: 4
Prep Time: 15 Minutes | Cooking Time: 25 Minutes
Ingredients:

- 4 crusty rolls
- 4 Gouda cheese thin slices
- 5 eggs
- 2 tbsp heavy cream
- 1/2 tsp dried thyme
- 3 Parma ham slices, chopped
- Salt and pepper to taste

Directions:

1. Preheat air fryer to 165°C/330°F.

2. Cut tops off rolls and hollow out leaving 1.3cm bread shell.

3. Line shells with cheese slices.

4. Beat eggs with cream. Add thyme, ham, salt and pepper.

5. Pour egg mixture into bread cups.

6. Place in greased air fryer basket.

7. Bake 8-12 mins until eggs are puffy and golden.

8. Serve warm.

9. **Variations & Ingredients Tips**:

10. Use different cheese like cheddar or swiss.

11. Add sauteed spinach, mushrooms or bell peppers.

12. Substitute turkey or cooked bacon for the ham.

13. **Per serving**: Calories: 270; Total Fat: 16g; Saturated Fat: 7g; Cholesterol: 250mg; Sodium: 580mg; Total Carbs: 18g; Dietary Fiber: 1g; Sugars: 2g; Protein: 15g

Mushroom & Cavolo Nero Egg Muffins

Servings: 6
Prep Time: 10 Minutes | Cooking Time: 20 Minutes
Ingredients:

- 225g baby Bella mushrooms, sliced
- 6 eggs, beaten
- 1 garlic clove, minced
- Salt and pepper to taste
- 1/2 tsp chili powder
- 1 cup cavolo nero (Tuscan kale), shredded
- 2 scallions, diced

Directions:

1. Preheat air fryer to 160°C/320°F.
2. Place eggs, garlic, salt, pepper and chili powder in a bowl and beat well combined.
3. Fold in mushrooms, cavolo nero and scallions.
4. Divide mixture between greased muffin cups and place in air fryer basket.
5. Bake for 12-15 minutes until eggs are set.
6. Cool 5 minutes before serving.
7. **Variations & Ingredients Tips**:
8. Use different greens like spinach or chard.
9. Add diced ham, bacon or cheese.
10. Cook in oven-safe ramekins if air fryer cups are too small.
11. **Per serving**: Calories: 75; Total Fat: 4g; Saturated Fat: 1g; Cholesterol: 155mg; Sodium: 90mg; Total Carbs: 4g; Dietary Fiber: 1g; Sugars: 2g; Protein: 6g

Cinnamon Rolls With Cream Cheese Glaze

Servings: 8
Prep Time: 20 Minutes | Cooking Time: 9 Minutes
Ingredients:

- 450 g frozen bread dough, thawed
- ¼ cup butter, melted and cooled
- ¾ cup brown sugar
- 1½ tablespoons ground cinnamon
- Cream Cheese Glaze:
- 113 g cream cheese, softened
- 2 tablespoons butter, softened
- 1¼ cups powdered sugar
- ½ teaspoon vanilla

Directions:

1. Let the bread dough come to room temperature on the counter. On a lightly floured surface roll the dough into a 33 cm by 28 cm rectangle. Position the rectangle so the 33 cm side is facing you. Brush the melted butter all over the dough, leaving a 2.5 cm border uncovered along the edge farthest away from you.
2. Combine the brown sugar and cinnamon in a small bowl. Sprinkle the mixture evenly over the buttered dough, keeping the 5 cm border uncovered. Roll the dough into a log starting with the edge closest to you. Roll the dough tightly, making sure to roll evenly and push out any air pockets. When you get to the uncovered edge of the dough, press the dough onto the roll to seal it together.
3. Cut the log into 8 pieces slicing slowly with a sawing motion so you don't flatten the dough. Turn the slices on their sides and cover with a clean kitchen towel. Let the rolls sit in the warmest part of your kitchen for 1½ to 2 hours to rise.
4. To make the glaze, place the cream cheese and butter in a microwave-safe bowl. Soften the mixture in the microwave for 30 seconds at a time until it is easy to stir. Gradually add the powdered sugar and stir to combine. Add the vanilla extract and whisk until smooth. Set aside.
5. When the rolls have risen, preheat the air fryer to 180°C/350°F.
6. Transfer 4 of the rolls to the air fryer basket. Air-fry for 5 minutes. Turn the rolls over and air-fry for another 4 minutes. Repeat with the remaining 4 rolls.
7. Let the rolls cool for a couple of minutes before glazing. Spread large dollops of cream cheese glaze on top of the warm cinnamon rolls, allowing some of the glaze to drip down the side of the rolls. Serve warm and enjoy!
8. **Variations & Ingredients Tips**:
9. Use different types of filling, such as chocolate or nuts, for a variety of flavors and textures.
10. Add some grated orange or lemon zest to the dough for extra flavor.
11. For a vegan version, use non-dairy butter and cream cheese in the dough and glaze.

12. **Per Serving**: Calories: 450; Total Fat: 20g; Saturated Fat: 11g; Cholesterol: 50mg; Sodium: 480mg; Total Carbs: 62g; Fiber: 2g; Sugars: 32g; Protein: 8g

Coconut Mini Tarts

Servings: 2
Prep Time: 10 Minutes | Cooking Time: 25 Minutes
Ingredients:
- ¼ cup almond butter
- 1 tablespoon coconut sugar
- 2 tablespoons coconut yogurt
- ½ cup oat flour
- 2 tablespoons strawberry jam

Directions:
1. Preheat air fryer to 180°C/350°F. Use 2 pieces of parchment paper, each 20 cm long. Draw a rectangle on one piece.
2. Beat the almond butter, coconut sugar, and coconut yogurt in a shallow bowl until well combined. Mix in oat flour until you get a dough.
3. Put the dough onto the undrawing paper and cover it with the other one, rectangle-side up. Using a rolling pin, roll out until you get a rectangle. Discard top paper.
4. Cut it into 4 equal rectangles. Spread on 2 rectangles, 1 tablespoon of strawberry jam each, then top with the remaining rectangles. Using a fork, press all edges to seal them.
5. Bake in the fryer for 8 minutes. Serve right away.
6. **Variations & Ingredients Tips**:
7. Use different types of nut butter, such as cashew or walnut butter, for a variety of flavors.
8. Add some shredded coconut or chopped nuts to the dough for extra texture.
9. For a savory version, replace the strawberry jam with pesto or hummus.
10. **Per Serving**: Calories: 350; Total Fat: 24g; Saturated Fat: 5g; Cholesterol: 0mg; Sodium: 60mg; Total Carbs: 30g; Fiber: 4g; Sugars: 12g; Protein: 9g

Zucchini Walnut Bread

Servings: 6
Prep Time: 15 Minutes | Cooking Time: 30 Minutes
Ingredients:
- ¾ cup all-purpose flour
- ½ teaspoon baking soda
- 1 teaspoon ground cinnamon
- ⅛ teaspoon salt
- 1 large egg
- ⅓ cup packed brown sugar
- ¼ cup canola oil
- 1 teaspoon vanilla extract
- ⅓ cup milk
- 1 medium zucchini, shredded (about 1⅓ cups)
- ⅓ cup chopped walnuts

Directions:
1. Preheat the air fryer to 160°C/320°F.
2. In a medium bowl, mix together the flour, baking soda, cinnamon, and salt.
3. In a large bowl, whisk together the egg, brown sugar, oil, vanilla, and milk. Stir in the zucchini.
4. Slowly fold the dry ingredients into the wet ingredients. Stir in the chopped walnuts. Then pour the batter into two 10-cm oven-safe loaf pans.
5. Bake for 30 minutes or until a toothpick inserted into the center comes out clean. Let cool before slicing.
6. NOTE: Store tightly wrapped on the counter for up to 5 days, in the refrigerator for up to 10 days, or in the freezer for 3 months.
7. **Variations & Ingredients Tips**:
8. Use whole wheat flour for a healthier twist.
9. Add some raisins or dried cranberries for extra sweetness and texture.
10. Sprinkle the top with cinnamon sugar before baking for a crunchy crust.
11. **Per serving**: Calories: 260; Total Fat: 14g; Saturated Fat: 1g; Cholesterol: 30mg; Sodium: 180mg; Total Carbohydrates: 31g; Dietary Fiber: 1g; Total Sugars: 17g; Protein: 4g

Crispy Bacon

Servings: 6
Prep Time: 5 Minutes | Cooking Time: 20 Minutes
Ingredients:
- 340 g bacon

Directions:
1. Preheat the air fryer to 180°C/350°F for 3 minutes.
2. Lay out the bacon in a single layer, slightly overlapping the strips of bacon.
3. Air fry for 10 minutes or until desired crispness.
4. Repeat until all the bacon has been cooked.
5. **Variations & Ingredients Tips**:

6. Use different types of bacon, such as turkey or Canadian bacon, for a variety of flavors.

7. Sprinkle some brown sugar or maple syrup on the bacon before cooking for a sweet and savory twist.

8. Serve the crispy bacon with a side of scrambled eggs or pancakes for a classic breakfast.

9. **Per Serving**: Calories: 130; Total Fat: 10g; Saturated Fat: 3.5g; Cholesterol: 25mg; Sodium: 380mg; Total Carbs: 0g; Fiber: 0g; Sugars: 0g; Protein: 8g

French Toast Sticks Recipes

Servings: 4
Prep Time: 10 Minutes | Cooking Time: 7 Minutes
Ingredients:
- 2 eggs
- 118 ml milk
- ⅛ teaspoon salt
- ½ teaspoon pure vanilla extract
- 177 ml crushed cornflakes
- 6 slices sandwich bread, each slice cut into 4 strips
- oil for misting or cooking spray
- maple syrup or honey

Directions:
1. In a small bowl, beat together eggs, milk, salt, and vanilla.

2. Place crushed cornflakes on a plate or in a shallow dish.

3. Dip bread strips in egg mixture, shake off excess, and roll in cornflake crumbs.

4. Spray both sides of bread strips with oil.

5. Place bread strips in air fryer basket in single layer.

6. Cook at 200°C/390°F for 7 minutes or until they're dark golden brown.

7. Repeat steps 5 and 6 to cook remaining French toast sticks.

8. Serve with maple syrup or honey for dipping.

9. **Variations & Ingredients Tips**:

10. Use cinnamon raisin bread or banana bread for a flavor twist.

11. Crush up frosted flakes, honey nut cheerios or graham crackers for the coating.

12. Dust with powdered sugar and cocoa powder for a churro-like treat.

13. **Per Serving**: Calories: 264; Total Fat: 7g; Saturated Fat: 2g; Cholesterol: 98mg; Sodium: 474mg;

Total Carbs: 40g; Dietary Fiber: 2g; Total Sugars: 8g; Protein: 10g

Morning Apple Biscuits

Servings: 6
Prep Time: 5 Minutes | Cooking Time: 15 Minutes
Ingredients:
- 1 apple, grated
- 1 cup oat flour
- 2 tbsp honey
- 1/4 cup peanut butter
- 1/3 cup raisins
- 1/2 tsp ground cinnamon

Directions:
1. Preheat air fryer to 175°C/350°F.

2. Combine apple, flour, honey, peanut butter, raisins and cinnamon in a bowl.

3. Form into balls and flatten slightly.

4. Place on parchment paper in air fryer basket.

5. Bake for 9 minutes until lightly browned.

6. Serve warm.

7. **Variations & Ingredients Tips**:

8. Use almond or cashew butter instead of peanut.

9. Add chopped nuts or chocolate chips.

10. Drizzle with maple syrup or dust with powdered sugar.

11. **Per Serving**: Calories: 140; Total Fat: 6g; Saturated Fat: 1g; Cholesterol: 0mg; Sodium: 45mg; 19g; Dietary Fiber: 3g; Sugars: 9g; Protein: 4g

Quesadillas

Servings: 4

Prep Time: 10 Minutes | Cooking Time: 12 Minutes

Ingredients:

- 4 eggs
- 2 tablespoons skim milk
- Salt and pepper
- Oil for misting or cooking spray
- 4 flour tortillas
- 4 tablespoons salsa
- 55g Cheddar cheese, grated
- 1/2 small avocado, peeled and thinly sliced

Directions:

1. Preheat air fryer to 135°C/270°F.
2. Beat together eggs, milk, salt and pepper.
3. Spray a 15x15cm air fryer baking pan lightly with cooking spray and add egg mixture.
4. Cook 9 mins, stirring every 1-2 mins, until eggs are scrambled. Remove and set aside.
5. Spray one side of each tortilla with oil or cooking spray. Flip over.
6. Divide eggs, salsa, cheese and avocado among tortillas, covering half of each.
7. Fold tortillas in half and press down lightly.
8. Place 2 tortillas in air fryer basket and cook at 200°C/390°F for 3 mins until crispy.
9. Repeat with remaining 2 tortillas.
10. Cut each quesadilla into halves or thirds before serving.
11. **Variations & Ingredients Tips**:
12. Add cooked chorizo, chicken or peppers to the filling.
13. Use whole wheat or veggie tortillas for extra nutrition.
14. Serve with sour cream, guacamole or pico de gallo on the side.
15. **Per serving**: Calories: 270; Total Fat: 14g; Saturated Fat: 4g; Cholesterol: 185mg; Sodium: 430mg; Total Carbs: 24g; Dietary Fiber: 3g; Sugars: 2g; Protein: 13g

Shakshuka Cups

Servings: 4

Prep Time: 10 Minutes | Cooking Time: 25 Minutes

Ingredients:

- 2 tbsp tomato paste
- ½ cup chicken broth
- 4 tomatoes, diced
- 2 garlic cloves, minced
- ½ tsp dried oregano
- ½ tsp dried coriander
- ½ tsp dried basil
- ¼ tsp red pepper flakes
- ¼ tsp paprika
- 4 eggs
- Salt and pepper to taste
- 2 scallions, diced
- ½ cup grated cheddar cheese
- ½ cup Parmesan cheese
- 4 bread slices, toasted

Directions:

1. Preheat air fryer to 180℃/350°F.
2. Combine the tomato paste, broth, tomatoes, garlic, oregano, coriander, basil, red pepper flakes, and paprika.
3. Pour mixture evenly into greased ramekins. Bake 5 minutes.
4. Carefully remove ramekins and crack one egg in each, season with salt and pepper.
5. Top with scallions, cheeses.
6. Return to fryer and bake 3-5 minutes until eggs are set and cheese melted.
7. Serve with toasted bread.
8. **Variations & Ingredients Tips**:
9. Use different cheese varieties like feta or goat cheese.
10. Add cooked chorizo or ground meat to the sauce.
11. Serve with pita bread or over rice.
12. **Per serving**: Calories: 269; Total Fat: 16g; Saturated Fat: 7g; Cholesterol: 216mg; Sodium: 746mg; Total Carbs: 15g; Dietary Fiber: 2g; Total Sugars: 6g; Protein: 17g

Pancake Muffins

Servings: 4
Prep Time: 20 Minutes | Cooking Time: 8 Minutes

Ingredients:

- 1 cup flour
- 2 tbsp sugar (optional)
- 1/2 tsp baking soda
- 1 tsp baking powder
- 1/4 tsp salt
- 1 egg, beaten
- 1 cup buttermilk
- 2 tbsp melted butter
- 1 tsp vanilla extract
- 24 foil muffin cups
- Cooking spray
- Filling Suggestions:
- 1 tsp jelly/fruit preserves
- 1 tbsp or less fresh/frozen berries
- Dark chocolate chips
- Chopped nuts
- Cooked crumbled bacon/sausage

Directions:

1. In a bowl, mix flour, sugar, baking soda, powder and salt.
2. In another bowl, whisk egg, buttermilk, butter and vanilla.
3. Pour wet into dry ingredients and mix gently.
4. Grease foil cups and place 6 sets in air fryer basket.
5. Pour some batter into cups. Top with fillings, then more batter to 3/4 full.
6. Cook at 165°C/330°F for 8 mins.
7. Repeat to make remaining muffins.
8. **Variations & Ingredients Tips**:
9. Use different milk like almond or oat milk.
10. Add shredded cheese or herbs to the batter.
11. Drizzle with maple syrup before serving.
12. **Per serving**: Calories: 170; Total Fat: 6g; Saturated Fat: 3g; Cholesterol: 40mg; Sodium: 270mg; Total Carbs: 24g; Dietary Fiber: 1g; Sugars: 5g; Protein: 4g

Parmesan Pizza Nuggets

Servings: 8
Prep Time: 20 Minutes | Cooking Time: 6 Minutes
Ingredients:

- ¾ cup warm filtered water
- 1 package fast-rising yeast
- ½ tsp salt
- 2 cups all-purpose flour
- ¼ cup finely grated Parmesan cheese
- 1 tsp Italian seasoning
- 2 tbsp extra-virgin olive oil
- 1 tsp kosher salt

Directions:

1. Preheat the air fryer to 190°C/370°F. In a large microwave-safe bowl, add the water. Heat for 40 seconds in the microwave. Remove and mix in the yeast and salt. Let sit 5 minutes. Meanwhile, in a medium bowl, mix the flour with the Parmesan cheese and Italian seasoning. Set aside. Using a stand mixer with a dough hook attachment, add the yeast liquid and then mix in the flour mixture ⅓ cup at a time until all the flour mixture is added and a dough is formed. Remove the bowl from the stand, and then let the dough rise for 1 hour in a warm space, covered with a kitchen towel. After the dough has doubled in size, remove it from the bowl and punch it down a few times on a lightly floured flat surface. Divide the dough into 4 balls, and then roll each ball out into a long, skinny, sticklike shape. Using a sharp knife, cut each dough stick into 6 pieces. Repeat for the remaining dough balls until you have about 24 nuggets formed. Lightly brush the top of each bite with the egg whites and cover with a pinch of sea salt. Spray the air fryer basket with olive oil spray and place the pizza nuggets on top. Cook for 6 minutes, or until lightly browned. Remove and keep warm. Repeat until all the nuggets are cooked. Serve warm.
2. **Variations & Ingredients Tips:**
3. Add finely chopped pepperoni, sausage, or veggies to the dough for a stuffed pizza nugget.
4. Serve with warm marinara sauce or ranch dressing for dipping.
5. Sprinkle with additional grated Parmesan cheese or Italian seasoning before serving.

6. **Per serving:** Calories: 157; Total Fat: 5g; Saturated Fat: 1g; Cholesterol: 1mg; Sodium: 372mg; Total Carbs: 24g; Dietary Fiber: 1g; Total Sugars: 0g; Protein: 5g

Parmesan Eggplant Bites

Servings: 4
Prep Time: 15 Minutes | Cooking Time: 35 Minutes
Ingredients:

- 2 eggs
- 2 tbsp heavy cream
- ½ cup bread crumbs
- ½ tsp Italian seasoning
- ½ cup grated Parmesan
- ½ tsp salt
- 1 eggplant, cut into sticks
- ½ cup tomato sauce, warm

Directions:

1. Preheat air fryer to 200°C/400°F. In a bowl, mix the eggs and heavy cream. In another bowl, combine bread crumbs, Parmesan cheese, Italian seasoning and salt. Dip eggplant fries in egg mixture and dredge them in crumb mixture. Place the fries in the greased frying basket and air fry for 12 minutes, shaking once. Transfer to a large serving plate and serve with warmed tomato sauce.
2. **Variations & Ingredients Tips:**
3. Use zucchini or yellow squash instead of eggplant for a different veggie option.
4. Add grated mozzarella or provolone cheese to the bread crumb mixture for extra cheesiness.
5. Serve with marinara sauce, pesto, or garlic aioli for dipping.
6. **Per serving:** Calories: 176; Total Fat: 9g; Saturated Fat: 4g; Cholesterol: 108mg; Sodium: 721mg; Total Carbs: 15g; Dietary Fiber: 4g; Total Sugars: 4g; Protein: 10g

Turkey Burger Sliders

Servings: 8
Prep Time: 10 Minutes | Cooking Time: 7 Minutes
Ingredients:

- 450 g ground turkey
- ¼ tsp curry powder
- 1 tsp Hoisin sauce
- ½ tsp salt
- 8 slider buns
- ½ cup slivered red onions
- ½ cup slivered green or red bell pepper
- ½ cup fresh chopped pineapple (or pineapple tidbits from kids' fruit cups, drained)
- light cream cheese, softened

Directions:

1. Combine turkey, curry powder, Hoisin sauce, and salt and mix together well. Shape turkey mixture into 8 small patties. Place patties in air fryer basket and cook at 180°C/360°F for 7 minutes, until patties are well done and juices run clear. Place each patty on the bottom half of a slider bun and top with onions, peppers, and pineapple. Spread the remaining bun halves with cream cheese to taste, place on top, and serve.
2. **Variations & Ingredients Tips**:
3. Add garlic powder, ginger, or soy sauce to the turkey mixture for an Asian-inspired flavor.
4. Top the sliders with sliced avocado, sriracha mayo, or pickled vegetables for extra toppings.
5. Use Hawaiian sweet rolls or pretzel buns instead of regular slider buns for a twist.
6. **Per Serving**: Calories: 200; Total Fat: 9g; Saturated Fat: 3g; Cholesterol: 56mg; Sodium: 326mg; Total Carbohydrates: 17g; Dietary Fiber: 1g; Total Sugars: 5g; Protein: 15g

Fried Bananas

Servings: 4
Prep Time: 15 Minutes | Cooking Time: 8 Minutes
Ingredients:
- ½ cup panko breadcrumbs
- ½ cup sweetened coconut flakes
- ¼ cup sliced almonds
- ½ cup cornstarch
- 2 egg whites
- 1 tablespoon water
- 2 firm bananas
- oil for misting or cooking spray

Directions:

1. In food processor, combine panko, coconut, and almonds. Process to make small crumbs.
2. Place cornstarch in a shallow dish. In another shallow dish, beat together the egg whites and water until slightly foamy.
3. Preheat air fryer to 200°C/390°F.
4. Cut bananas in half crosswise. Cut each half in quarters lengthwise so you have 16 "sticks."
5. Dip banana sticks in cornstarch and tap to shake off excess. Then dip bananas in egg wash and roll in crumb mixture. Spray with oil.
6. Place bananas in air fryer basket in single layer and cook for 4 minutes. If any spots have not browned, spritz with oil. Cook for 4 more minutes, until golden brown and crispy.
7. Repeat step 6 to cook remaining bananas.
8. **Variations & Ingredients Tips**:
9. Use plantains instead of bananas for a less sweet version.
10. Add some cinnamon, nutmeg or vanilla extract to the crumb mixture.
11. Serve with chocolate sauce, dulce de leche or fruit compote for dipping.
12. **Per serving**: Calories: 306; Total Fat: 11g; Saturated Fat: 5g; Cholesterol: 0mg; Sodium: 148mg; Total Carbs: 48g; Dietary Fiber: 4g; Total Sugars: 17g; Protein: 6g

Italian Bruschetta With Mushrooms & Cheese

Servings: 4
Prep Time: 10 Minutes | Cooking Time: 25 Minutes
Ingredients:
- ½ cup button mushrooms, chopped
- ½ baguette, sliced
- 1 garlic clove, minced
- 85 g sliced Parmesan cheese
- 1 tbsp extra virgin olive oil
- Salt and pepper to taste

Directions:

1. Preheat air fryer to 175°C/350°F. Add the mushrooms, olive oil, salt, pepper, and garlic to a mixing bowl and stir thoroughly to combine. Divide the mushroom mixture between the bread slices, drizzling all over the surface with olive oil, then cover with Parmesan slices. Place the covered bread slices in the

greased frying basket and Bake for 15 minutes. Serve and enjoy!

2. **Variations & Ingredients Tips**:

3. Use ciabatta, sourdough or focaccia bread instead of baguette.

4. Top with mozzarella, fontina or gorgonzola cheese in addition to Parmesan.

5. Add some chopped tomatoes, basil or balsamic glaze before serving.

6. **Per serving**: Calories: 220; Total Fat: 12g; Saturated Fat: 5g; Cholesterol: 19mg; Sodium: 508mg; Total Carbs: 18g; Dietary Fiber: 1g; Total Sugars: 1g; Protein: 11g

Tomato & Halloumi Bruschetta

Servings: 4

Prep Time: 10 Minutes | Cooking Time: 20 Minutes

Ingredients:

- 2 tbsp softened butter
- 8 French bread slices
- 1 cup grated halloumi cheese
- ½ cup basil pesto
- 12 chopped cherry tomatoes
- 2 green onions, thinly sliced

Directions:

1. Preheat air fryer to 175°C/350°F. Spread butter on one side of the bread. Place butter-side up in the frying basket. Bake until the bread is slightly brown, 3-5 minutes. Remove the bread and top it with halloumi cheese. Melt the cheese on the bread in the air fryer for another 1-3 minutes. Meanwhile, mix pesto, cherry tomatoes, and green onions in a small bowl. When the cheese has melted, take the bread out of the fryer and arrange on a plate. Top with pesto mix and serve.

2. **Variations & Ingredients Tips**:

3. Use feta, goat cheese, or mozzarella instead of halloumi for a different cheese option.

4. Add chopped olives, sun-dried tomatoes, or roasted red peppers to the tomato mixture for a Mediterranean flair.

5. Drizzle with balsamic glaze or olive oil before serving for extra richness.

6. **Per Serving**: Calories: 347; Total Fat: 23g; Saturated Fat: 11g; Cholesterol: 49mg; Sodium: 741mg; Total Carbohydrates: 24g; Dietary Fiber: 2g; Total Sugars: 3g; Protein: 14g

Cheddar-pimiento Strips

Prep Time: 15 Minutes | Servings: 4

Cooking Time: 35 Minutes

Ingredients:

- 225 g shredded sharp cheddar cheese
- 1 jar chopped pimientos, including juice
- ¼ cup mayonnaise
- ¼ cup cream cheese
- Salt and pepper to taste
- 1 tsp chopped parsley
- 8 slices sandwich bread
- 4 tbsp butter, melted

Directions:

1. In a bowl, mix the cheddar cheese, cream cheese, pimientos, mayonnaise, salt, parsley and pepper. Let chill covered in the fridge for 30 minutes.

2. Preheat air fryer at 175°C/350°F. Spread pimiento mixture over 4 bread slices, then top with the remaining slices and press down just enough to not smoosh cheese out of sandwiches edges. Brush the top and bottom of each sandwich lightly with melted butter. Place sandwiches in the frying basket and Grill for 6 minutes, flipping once. Slice each sandwich into 16 sections and serve warm.

3. **Variations & Ingredients Tips**:

4. Use sourdough or rye bread for a tangy flavor.

5. Add some chopped green onions or diced jalapenos to the cheese mixture.

6. Serve with tomato soup or a green salad on the side.

7. **Per serving**: Calories: 609; Total Fat: 46g; Saturated Fat: 25g; Cholesterol: 97mg; Sodium: 1040mg; Total Carbs: 30g; Dietary Fiber: 2g; Total Sugars: 5g; Protein: 22g

Mozzarella Sticks

Servings: 4

Prep Time: 10 Minutes | Cooking Time: 5 Minutes

Ingredients:

- 1 egg
- 1 tbsp water
- 8 eggroll wraps
- 8 mozzarella string cheese "sticks"
- sauce for dipping

Directions:

1. Beat together egg and water in a small bowl. Lay out egg roll wraps and moisten edges with egg wash. Place one piece of string cheese on each wrap near one end. Fold in sides of egg roll wrap over ends of cheese, and then roll up. Brush outside of wrap with egg wash and press gently to seal well. Place in air fryer basket in single layer and cook at 200°C/390°F for 5 minutes. Cook an additional 1 or 2 minutes, if necessary, until they are golden brown and crispy. Serve with your favorite dipping sauce.

2. **Variations & Ingredients Tips**:

3. Use wonton wrappers instead of egg roll wraps for a lighter, crispier texture.

4. Experiment with different types of cheese like cheddar, pepper jack, or gouda.

5. Serve with ranch dressing, marinara sauce, or garlic aioli for dipping.

6. **Per serving**: Calories: 218; Total Fat: 9g; Saturated Fat: 4g; Cholesterol: 71mg; Sodium: 552mg; Total Carbs: 23g; Dietary Fiber: 1g; Total Sugars: 1g; Protein: 12g

Fried Gyoza

Servings: 18
Prep Time: 20 Minutes | Cooking Time: 6 Minutes
Ingredients:

* 140 g Lean ground pork
* 2½ tablespoons Very thinly sliced scallion
* 1 tablespoon plus 2 teaspoons Minced peeled fresh ginger
* 1¼ teaspoons Toasted sesame oil
* ⅛ teaspoon Table salt
* ⅛ teaspoon Ground black pepper
* 18 Round gyoza or square wonton wrappers (thawed, if necessary)
* Vegetable oil spray

Directions:

1. Preheat the air fryer to 175°C/350°F.
2. Mix the ground pork, scallion, ginger, sesame oil, salt, and pepper in a bowl until well combined.
3. Set a bowl of water on a clean, dry surface or next to a clean, dry cutting board. Set one gyoza or wonton wrapper on that surface. Dip your clean finger in the water and run it around the perimeter of the gyoza wrapper or the edge of the wonton wrapper. Put about

1 ½ teaspoons of the meat mixture in the center of the wrapper.

4. For the gyoza wrapper, fold the wrapper in half to close, pressing the edge to seal, then wet the outside of the edge of both sides of the seam and pleat it into little ridges to seal.

5. For the wonton wrapper, fold it in half lengthwise to make a rectangle, then seal the sides together, flattening the packet a bit as you do.

6. Set the filled wrapper aside and continue making more in the same way. When done, generously coat them on all sides with vegetable oil spray.

7. Place the gyoza in the basket in one layer and air-fry undisturbed for 6 minutes, or until browned and crisp at the edges.

8. Use kitchen tongs or a nonstick-safe spatula to gently transfer the gyoza to a wire rack. Cool for only 2 or 3 minutes before serving hot.

9. **Variations & Ingredients Tips**:

10. Use ground chicken, turkey or shrimp instead of pork.

11. Add some shredded cabbage, carrots or mushrooms to the filling.

12. Serve with soy sauce, rice vinegar and chili oil for dipping.

13. **Per serving**: Calories: 54; Total Fat: 2g; Saturated Fat: 1g; Cholesterol: 8mg; Sodium: 87mg; Total Carbs: 5g; Dietary Fiber: 0g; Total Sugars: 0g; Protein: 3g

Crunchy Parmesan Edamame

Servings:4
Prep Time: 5 Minutes | Cooking Time: 25 Minutes + Cooling Time
Ingredients:

* 1 cup edamame, shelled
* 1 tbsp sesame oil
* 1 tsp five-spice powder
* ½ tsp salt
* ½ tsp garlic powder
* ¼ cup grated Parmesan

Directions:

1. Cook the edamame in boiling salted water until crisp-tender, about 10 minutes. Drain and leave to cool. Preheat air fryer to 175°C/350°F. Combine edamame, garlic, and sesame oil in a bowl. Place them in the frying basket and Air Fry for 16 minutes, shaking twice. Transfer to a small bowl and toss with five-spice

powder and salt. Serve chilled topped with Parmesan cheese. Enjoy!

2. **Variations & Ingredients Tips**:

3. Use frozen shelled edamame for convenience.

4. Substitute soy sauce or tamari for the salt.

5. Sprinkle with toasted sesame seeds or furikake seasoning.

6. **Per serving**: Calories: 127; Total Fat: 8g; Saturated Fat: 2g; Cholesterol: 4mg; Sodium: 405mg; Total Carbs: 8g; Dietary Fiber: 3g; Total Sugars: 2g; Protein: 7g

Hot Cheese Bites

Servings: 6

Prep Time: 15 Minutes | Cooking Time: 30 Minutes + Cooling Time

Ingredients:

- 1/3 cup grated Velveeta cheese
- 1/3 cup shredded American cheese
- 113 g cream cheese
- 2 jalapeños, finely chopped
- ½ cup bread crumbs
- 2 egg whites
- ½ cup all-purpose flour

Directions:

1. Preheat air fryer to 200°C/400°F. Blend the cream cheese, Velveeta, American cheese, and jalapeños in a bowl. Form the mixture into 2.5 cm balls. Arrange them on a sheet pan and freeze for 15 minutes.

2. Spread the flour, egg, and bread crumbs in 3 separate bowls. Once the cheese balls are removed from the freezer, dip them first in flour, then in the egg and finally in the crumbs. Air Fry for 8 minutes in the previously greased frying basket. Flip the balls and cook for another 4 minutes until crispy. Serve warm.

3. **Variations & Ingredients Tips**:

4. Use pepper jack, cheddar or mozzarella cheese for different flavors.

5. Add some chopped bacon, ham or chorizo to the cheese mixture.

6. Serve with ranch dressing, marinara sauce or salsa for dipping.

7. **Per serving**: Calories: 211; Total Fat: 13g; Saturated Fat: 7g; Cholesterol: 44mg; Sodium: 556mg; Total Carbs: 14g; Dietary Fiber: 1g; Total Sugars: 2g; Protein: 10g

Home-style Taro Chips

Servings: 2

Prep Time: 5 Minutes | Cooking Time: 20 Minutes

Ingredients:

- 1 tbsp olive oil
- 1 cup thinly sliced taro
- Salt to taste
- ½ cup hummus

Directions:

1. Preheat air fryer to 165°C/325°F. Put the sliced taro in the greased frying basket, spread the pieces out, and drizzle with olive oil. Air Fry for 10-12 minutes, shaking the basket twice. Sprinkle with salt and serve with hummus.

2. **Variations & Ingredients Tips**:

3. Use other root vegetables like sweet potatoes, beets or parsnips.

4. Season the chips with garlic powder, smoked paprika or curry powder.

5. Serve with guacamole, salsa or baba ghanoush for dipping.

6. **Per serving**: Calories: 236; Total Fat: 15g; Saturated Fat: 2g; Cholesterol: 0mg; Sodium: 308mg; Total Carbs: 25g; Dietary Fiber: 5g; Total Sugars: 3g; Protein: 5g

Apple Rollups

Servings: 8

Prep Time: 10 Minutes | Cooking Time: 5 Minutes

Ingredients:

- 8 slices whole wheat sandwich bread
- 113 g Colby Jack cheese, grated
- ½ small apple, chopped
- 2 tablespoons butter, melted

Directions:

1. Remove crusts from bread and flatten the slices with rolling pin. Don't be gentle. Press hard so that bread will be very thin.

2. Top bread slices with cheese and chopped apple, dividing the ingredients evenly.

3. Roll up each slice tightly and secure each with one or two toothpicks.

4. Brush outside of rolls with melted butter.

5. Place in air fryer basket and cook at 200°C/390°F for 5 minutes, until outside is crisp and nicely browned.

6. **Variations & Ingredients Tips**:
7. Try different cheeses like cheddar, brie or goat cheese.
8. Substitute pears or peaches for the apples.
9. Sprinkle with cinnamon-sugar before cooking for a sweet twist.
10. **Per Serving**: Calories: 169; Cholesterol: 19 mg; Total Fat: 10g; Saturated Fat: 6g: Sodium: 245mg; Total Carbohydrates: 16 g; Dietary Fiber: 2g; Total Sugars: 4 g; Protein: 7 g

Crab Toasts

Servings: 15
Prep Time: 10 Minutes | Cooking Time: 5 Minutes
Ingredients:
- 1 170 g can flaked crabmeat, well drained
- 3 tablespoons light mayonnaise
- ½ teaspoon lemon juice
- 1 teaspoon Worcestershire sauce
- ¼ cup shredded sharp Cheddar cheese
- ¼ cup shredded Parmesan cheese
- 1 loaf artisan bread, French bread, or baguette, cut into slices 10 mm thick

Directions:
1. Mix together all ingredients except the bread slices.
2. Spread each slice of bread with a thin layer of crabmeat mixture. (For a bread slice measuring 5 x 4 cm you will need about ½ tablespoon of crab mixture.)
3. Place in air fryer basket in single layer and cook at 180°C/360°F for 5 minutes or until tops brown and toast is crispy.
4. Repeat step 3 to cook remaining crab toasts.
5. **Variations & Ingredients Tips**:
6. Use smoked salmon, cooked shrimp or lobster instead of crab.
7. Add some minced jalapeños or hot sauce to the mixture for a spicy kick.
8. Sprinkle with Old Bay seasoning or smoked paprika before cooking.
9. **Per serving**: Calories: 104; Total Fat: 4g; Saturated Fat: 1g; Cholesterol: 17mg; Sodium: 271mg; Total Carbs: 12g; Dietary Fiber: 1g; Total Sugars: 1g; Protein: 5g

Sweet-and-salty Pretzels

Servings: 4

Prep Time: 5 Minutes | Cooking Time: 5 Minutes
Ingredients:
- 2 cups plain pretzel nuggets
- 1 tbsp Worcestershire sauce
- 2 tsp granulated white sugar
- 1 tsp mild smoked paprika
- ½ tsp garlic or onion powder

Directions:
1. Preheat the air fryer to 175°C/350°F. Put the pretzel nuggets, Worcestershire sauce, sugar, smoked paprika, and garlic or onion powder in a large bowl. Toss gently until the nuggets are well coated. When the machine is at temperature, pour the nuggets into the basket, spreading them into as close to a single layer as possible. Air-fry, shaking the basket three or four times to rearrange the nuggets, for 5 minutes, or until the nuggets are toasted and aromatic. Although the coating will darken, don't let it burn, especially if the machine's temperature is 180°C/360°F. Pour the nuggets onto a wire rack and gently spread them into one layer. (A rubber spatula does a good job.) Cool for 5 minutes before serving.
2. **Variations & Ingredients Tips**:
3. Experiment with different spice blends like ranch seasoning, taco seasoning, or Italian herbs.
4. Add a pinch of cayenne pepper or red pepper flakes for a spicy kick.
5. Drizzle with melted chocolate or caramel for a sweet and salty treat.
6. **Per Serving**: Calories: 113; Total Fat: 1g; Saturated Fat: 0g; Sodium: 504mg; Total Carbohydrates: 24g; Dietary Fiber: 1g; Total Sugars: 3g; Protein: 3g

Spicy Chicken And Pepper Jack Cheese Bites

Servings: 8
Prep Time: 20 Minutes + Chilling Time | Cooking Time: 8 Minutes
Ingredients:
- 225 g cream cheese, softened
- 2 cups grated pepper jack cheese
- 1 jalapeño pepper, diced
- 2 scallions, minced
- 1 tsp paprika
- 2 tsp salt, divided
- 3 cups shredded cooked chicken

- ¼ cup all-purpose flour*
- 2 eggs, lightly beaten
- 1 cup panko breadcrumbs*
- olive oil, in a spray bottle
- salsa

Directions:

1. Beat the cream cheese in a bowl until it is smooth and easy to stir. Add the pepper jack cheese, jalapeño pepper, scallions, paprika and 1 teaspoon of salt. Fold in the shredded cooked chicken and combine well. Roll this mixture into 2.5-cm balls. Set up a dredging station with three shallow dishes. Place the flour into one shallow dish. Place the eggs into a second shallow dish. Finally, combine the panko breadcrumbs and remaining teaspoon of salt in a third dish. Coat the chicken cheese balls by rolling each ball in the flour first, then dip them into the eggs and finally roll them in the panko breadcrumbs to coat all sides. Refrigerate for at least 30 minutes. Preheat the air fryer to 200°C/400°F. Spray the chicken cheese balls with oil and air-fry in batches for 8 minutes. Shake the basket a few times throughout the cooking process to help the balls brown evenly. Serve hot with salsa on the side.

2. **Variations & Ingredients Tips**:

3. Use a mixture of cheddar, mozzarella, and Parmesan cheese for a milder flavor.

4. Add chopped bacon, ham, or chorizo for a meatier bite.

5. Serve with ranch dressing, honey mustard, or BBQ sauce for dipping.

6. **Per Serving**: Calories: 341; Total Fat: 24g; Saturated Fat: 12g; Cholesterol: 143mg; Sodium: 892mg; Total Carbohydrates: 9g; Dietary Fiber: 1g; Total Sugars: 1g; Protein: 23g

- ½ tsp chili powder
- ¼ tsp ground cumin
- 1 tbsp dried Italian herbs
- ½ cup Parmesan cheese

Directions:

1. Preheat air fryer to 200°C/400°F. Cut off garlic head top and drizzle with olive oil. Wrap loosely in foil and transfer to the frying basket. Cook for 30 minutes. Remove from air fryer and open the foil. Cool the garlic for 10 minutes, then squeeze the cloves out of their place in the head. Chop and transfer all but ½ teaspoon to a small bowl. Stir in mayonnaise, lemon juice, Worcestershire, and cayenne pepper. Cover and refrigerate. Toss potatoes with the rest of the olive oil as well as salt, black pepper, Italian herbs, Parmesan cheese, chili powder, cumin, and the remaining chopped garlic. When coated, place the wedges in the frying basket in a single layer. Air fry for 10 minutes, then shake the basket. Air fry for another 8-10 minutes until potatoes are tender. Bring out the garlic aioli. Place the potato wedges on a serving dish along with the aioli for dipping. Serve warm.

2. **Variations & Ingredients Tips**:

3. Experiment with different potatoes like sweet potatoes, Yukon Gold, or red potatoes for varied flavors and textures.

4. Add chopped fresh herbs like rosemary, thyme, or parsley to the potatoes before cooking for extra aroma.

5. Serve with different dipping sauces like ranch, blue cheese, or chipotle mayo for variety.

6. **Per Serving**: Calories: 331; Total Fat: 24g; Saturated Fat: 5g; Cholesterol: 13mg; Sodium: 320mg; Total Carbohydrates: 25g; Dietary Fiber: 3g; Total Sugars: 1g; Protein: 7g

Uncle's Potato Wedges

Servings: 4
Prep Time: 15 Minutes | Cooking Time: 65 Minutes
Ingredients:

- 2 russet potatoes, cut into wedges
- 1 head garlic
- 3 tbsp olive oil
- ¼ cup mayonnaise
- ½ tbsp lemon juice
- ½ tsp Worcestershire sauce
- ⅛ tsp cayenne pepper
- Salt and pepper to taste

Olive & Pepper Tapenade

Servings: 4
Prep Time: 10 Minutes | Cooking Time: 10 Minutes
Ingredients:

- 1 red bell pepper
- 3 tbsp olive oil
- ½ cup black olives, chopped
- 1 garlic clove, minced
- ½ tsp dried oregano
- 1 tbsp white wine juice

Directions:

1. Preheat air fryer to 190°C/380°F. Lightly brush the outside of the bell pepper with some olive oil and put it in the frying basket. Roast for 5 minutes. Combine the remaining olive oil with olives, garlic, oregano, and white wine in a bowl. Remove the red pepper from the air fryer, then gently slice off the stem and discard the seeds. Chop into small pieces. Add the chopped pepper to the olive mixture and stir all together until combined. Serve and enjoy!

2. **Variations & Ingredients Tips**:

3. Use green olives or a mixture of olives for a different flavor profile.

4. Add anchovies or capers for a salty, briny kick.

5. Serve with crostini, pita chips, or fresh vegetables for dipping.

6. **Per serving**: Calories: 137; Total Fat: 14g; Saturated Fat: 2g; Cholesterol: no data; Sodium: 204mg; Total Carbs: 4g; Dietary Fiber: 1g; Total Sugars: 1g; Protein: 1g

Honey-lemon Chicken Wings

Servings: 4

Prep Time: 10 Minutes | Cooking Time: 30 Minutes

Ingredients:

- 8 chicken wings
- Salt and pepper to taste
- 3 tbsp honey
- 1 tbsp lemon juice
- 1 tbsp chicken stock
- 2 cloves garlic, minced
- 2 thinly sliced green onions
- ¾ cup barbecue sauce
- 1 tbsp sesame seeds

Directions:

1. Preheat air fryer to 200°C/390°F. Season the wings with salt and pepper and place them in the frying basket. Air Fry for 20 minutes. Shake the basket a couple of times during cooking. In a bowl, mix the honey, lemon juice, chicken stock, and garlic. Take the wings out of the fryer and place them in a baking pan. Add the sauce and toss, coating completely. Put the pan in the air fryer and Air Fry for 4-5 minutes until golden and cooked through, with no pink showing. Top with green onions and sesame seeds, then serve with BBQ sauce.

2. **Variations & Ingredients Tips**:

3. Use orange juice and zest instead of lemon for a different citrus flavor.

4. Add some sriracha or hot sauce to the honey mixture for spicy wings.

5. Garnish with chopped cilantro or parsley before serving.

6. **Per serving**: Calories: 331; Total Fat: 19g; Saturated Fat: 5g; Cholesterol: 48mg; Sodium: 627mg; Total Carbs: 27g; Dietary Fiber: 1g; Total Sugars: 23g; Protein: 14g

Cayenne-spiced Roasted Pecans

Servings: 4

Prep Time: 5 Minutes | Cooking Time: 15 Minutes

Ingredients:

- ¼ tsp chili powder
- Salt and pepper to taste
- ⅛ tsp cayenne pepper
- 1 tsp cumin powder
- 1 tsp cinnamon powder
- ⅛ tsp garlic powder
- ⅛ tsp onion powder
- 1 cup raw pecans
- 2 tbsp butter, melted
- 1 tsp honey

Directions:

1. Preheat air fryer to 150°C/300°F. Whisk together black pepper, chili powder, salt, cayenne pepper, cumin, garlic powder, cinnamon, and onion powder. Set to the side. Toss pecans, butter, and honey in a medium bowl, then toss in the spice mixture. Pour pecans in the frying basket and toast for 3 minutes. Stir the pecans and toast for another 3 to 5 minutes until the nuts are crisp. Cool and serve.

2. **Variations & Ingredients Tips**:

3. Use a mix of nuts like almonds, cashews and walnuts.

4. Add some brown sugar or maple syrup for a sweet and spicy combo.

5. Serve over salads, oatmeal or yogurt parfaits.

6. **Per serving**: Calories: 259; Total Fat: 26g; Saturated Fat: 6g; Cholesterol: 16mg; Sodium: 102mg; Total Carbs: 8g; Dietary Fiber: 4g; Total Sugars: 4g; Protein: 3g

Restaurant-style Chicken Thighs

Servings: 4
Prep Time: 5 Minutes (plus 10 Minutes Marinating Time) | Cooking Time: 30 Minutes
Ingredients:

- 454 grams boneless, skinless chicken thighs
- ¼ cup barbecue sauce
- 2 cloves garlic, minced
- 1 tsp lemon zest
- 2 tbsp parsley, chopped
- 2 tbsp lemon juice

Directions:
1. Coat the chicken with barbecue sauce, garlic, and lemon juice in a medium bowl. leave to marinate for 10 minutes.
2. Preheat air fryer to 190°C/380°F.
3. When ready to cook, remove the chicken from the bowl and shake off any drips. Arrange the chicken in the air fryer and Bake for 16-18 minutes, until golden and cooked through.
4. Serve topped with lemon zest and parsley. Enjoy!
5. **Variations & Ingredients Tips:**
6. Use honey mustard, teriyaki, or pesto sauce instead of BBQ for different flavors.
7. Add sliced onions, peppers, or mushrooms to the marinade for extra veggies.
8. Serve with sweet potato fries, coleslaw, or grilled corn on the side.
9. **Per Serving**: Calories: 250; Total Fat: 11g; Saturated Fat: 2.5g; Sodium: 440mg; Total Carbohydrates: 8g; Dietary Fiber: 0g; Total Sugars: 6g; Protein: 29g

Favorite Fried Chicken Wings

Servings: 4
Prep Time: 15 Minutes | Cooking Time: 30 Minutes
Ingredients:

- 16 chicken wings
- 1 tsp garlic powder
- 1/2 tsp paprika
- 1 tsp chicken seasoning
- Black pepper to taste
- 1/2 cup flour
- 1/4 cup sour cream
- 2 tsp red chili flakes

Directions:
1. Preheat air fryer to 200°C/400°F.
2. Put the drumettes in a resealable bag along with garlic powder, chicken seasoning, paprika, and pepper. Seal the bag and shake until the chicken is completely coated.
3. Prepare a clean resealable bag and add the flour. Pour sour cream in a large bowl.
4. Dunk the drumettes into the sour cream, then transfer them to the bag of flour. Seal the bag and shake until coated and repeat until all of the wings are coated.
5. Transfer the drumettes to the frying basket. Lightly spray them with cooking oil and Air Fry for 23-25 minutes, shaking the basket a few times until crispy and golden brown.
6. Allow to cool slightly. Sprinkle with red chili flakes and serve.
7. **Variations & Ingredients Tips:**
8. Toss the cooked wings in your favorite wing sauce like Buffalo or BBQ.
9. Marinate the wings overnight in buttermilk for extra tenderness.
10. Serve with celery sticks and blue cheese dressing.
11. **Per serving**: Calories: 470; Total Fat: 32g; Saturated Fat: 10g; Cholesterol: 155mg; Sodium: 620mg; Total Carbs: 14g; Dietary Fiber: 1g; Total Sugars: 1g; Protein: 33g

Cajun Fried Chicken

Servings: 3
Prep Time: 10 Minutes | Cooking Time: 35 Minutes
Ingredients:

- 1 cup Cajun seasoning
- ½ tsp mango powder
- 6 chicken legs, bone-in

Directions:
1. Preheat air fryer to 180°C/360°F.

2. Place half of the Cajun seasoning and 3/4 cup of water in a bowl and mix well to dissolve any lumps.

3. Add the remaining Cajun seasoning and mango powder to a shallow bowl and stir to combine.

4. Dip the chicken in the batter, then coat it in the mango seasoning. Lightly spritz the chicken with cooking spray.

5. Place the chicken in the air fryer and Air Fry for 14-16 minutes, turning once until the chicken is cooked and the coating is brown.

6. Serve and enjoy!

7. **Variations & Ingredients Tips**:

8. Use chicken wings, thighs, or breasts instead of legs.

9. Adjust the amount of Cajun seasoning to make it spicier or milder.

10. Serve with a side of coleslaw, potato salad, or corn on the cob.

11. **Per Serving**: Calories: 460; Total Fat: 26g; Saturated Fat: 7g; Sodium: 2270mg; Total Carbohydrates: 9g; Dietary Fiber: 3g; Total Sugars: 1g; Protein: 45g

Chicken Hand Pies

Servings: 8
Prep Time: 20 Minutes | Cooking Time: 10 Minutes Per Batch

Ingredients:

- 3/4 cup chicken broth
- 3/4 cup frozen mixed peas and carrots
- 1 cup cooked chicken, chopped
- 1 tablespoon cornstarch
- 1 tablespoon milk
- Salt and pepper
- 1 8-count can organic flaky biscuits
- Oil for misting or cooking spray

Directions:

1. In a saucepan, bring broth to a boil. Add peas, carrots and chicken.

2. Mix cornstarch and milk, then stir into broth mixture until thickened.

3. Remove from heat, season with salt and pepper, and let cool slightly.

4. Separate biscuits into 16 rounds, flattening each slightly.

5. Place filling on 8 biscuit rounds. Top with remaining rounds and crimp edges sealed.

6. Mist both sides with oil or cooking spray.

7. Air fry in batches at 165°C/330°F for 10 minutes until golden brown.

8. **Variations & Ingredients Tips**:

9. Use rotisserie or leftover chicken.

10. Add diced potatoes, celery or onions to the filling.

11. Brush with egg wash before cooking for a shiny finish.

12. **Per Serving** (2 hand pies): Calories: 312; Total Fat: 11g; Saturated Fat: 3g; Cholesterol: 38mg; Sodium: 779mg; Total Carbs: 41g; Dietary Fiber: 3g; Total Sugars: 4g; Protein: 13g

Mumbai Chicken Nuggets

Servings: 4
Prep Time: 15 Minutes | Cooking Time: 30 Minutes

Ingredients:

- 450g boneless, skinless chicken breasts
- 4 tsp curry powder
- Salt and pepper to taste
- 1 egg, beaten
- 2 tbsp sesame oil
- 1 cup panko bread crumbs
- 1/2 cup coconut yogurt
- 1/3 cup mango chutney
- 1/4 cup mayonnaise

Directions:

1. Preheat the air fryer to 200°C/400°F.

2. Cube the chicken into 5-cm pieces and sprinkle with 3 tsp of curry powder, salt, and pepper; toss to coat.

3. Beat together the egg and sesame oil in a shallow bowl and scatter the panko onto a separate plate. Dip the chicken in the egg, then in the panko, and press to coat. Lay the coated nuggets on a wire rack as you work.

4. Set the nuggets in the greased frying basket and Air Fry for 7-10 minutes, rearranging once halfway through cooking.

5. While the nuggets are cooking, combine the yogurt, chutney, mayonnaise, and the remaining teaspoon of curry powder in a small bowl.

6. Serve the nuggets with the dipping sauce.

7. **Variations & Ingredients Tips**:

8. Use Greek yogurt instead of coconut yogurt for a tangy dip.

9. Add some garam masala or cumin to the breading for extra flavor.

10. Serve nuggets in naan bread or roti wraps with shredded veggies.

11. **Per serving**: Calories: 450; Total Fat: 22g; Saturated Fat: 5g; Cholesterol: 150mg; Sodium: 470mg; Total Carbs: 30g; Dietary Fiber: 2g; Total Sugars: 15g; Protein: 36g

Tuscan Stuffed Chicken

Servings: 4
Prep Time: 15 Minutes | Cooking Time: 30 Minutes
Ingredients:

- 1/3 cup ricotta cheese
- 1 cup Tuscan kale, chopped
- 4 chicken breasts
- 1 tbsp chicken seasoning
- Salt and pepper to taste
- 1 tsp paprika

Directions:

1. Preheat air fryer to 190°C/370°F.
2. Soften the ricotta cheese in a microwave-safe bowl for 15 seconds. Combine in a bowl along with Tuscan kale. Set aside.
3. Cut 4-5 slits in the top of each chicken breast about 3/4 of the way down. Season with chicken seasoning, salt, and pepper.
4. Place the chicken with the slits facing up in the greased frying basket. Lightly spray the chicken with oil. Bake for 6-8 minutes.
5. Slide-out and stuff the cream cheese mixture into the chicken slits. Sprinkle 1/2 tsp of paprika and cook for another 3 minutes.
6. Serve and enjoy!
7. **Variations & Ingredients Tips**:
8. Use spinach, sun-dried tomatoes or roasted red peppers instead of kale.
9. Mix some pesto or minced garlic into the ricotta.
10. Sprinkle with grated Parmesan before serving.
11. **Per serving**: Calories: 270; Total Fat: 11g; Saturated Fat: 5g; Cholesterol: 125mg; Sodium: 530mg; Total Carbs: 2g; Dietary Fiber: 0g; Total Sugars: 1g; Protein: 39g

Fancy Chicken Piccata

Servings: 4
Prep Time: 20 Minutes | Cooking Time: 30 Minutes
Ingredients:

- 450g chicken breasts, cut into cutlets
- Salt and pepper to taste
- 2 egg whites
- 2/3 cup bread crumbs
- 1 tsp Italian seasoning
- 1 tbsp whipped butter
- 1/2 cup chicken broth
- 1/2 tsp onion powder
- 1/4 cup fino sherry
- Juice of 1 lemon
- 1 tbsp capers, drained
- 1 lemon, sliced
- 2 tbsp chopped parsley

Directions:

1. Preheat air fryer to 190°C/370°F.
2. Place the cutlets between two sheets of parchment paper. Pound to a 6-mm thickness and season with salt and pepper.
3. Beat egg whites with 1 tsp of water in a bowl. Put the bread crumbs, onion powder, and Italian seasoning in a second bowl.
4. Dip the cutlet in the egg bowl, and then in the crumb mix. Put the cutlets in the greased frying basket. Air Fry for 6 minutes, flipping once until crispy and golden.
5. Melt butter in a skillet. Stir in broth, sherry, lemon juice, lemon halves, and black pepper. Bring to a boil over high heat until the sauce is reduced by half, 4 minutes.
6. Remove from heat. Pick out the lemon rinds and discard them. Stir in capers.
7. Plate a cutlet, spoon some sauce over and garnish with lemon slices and parsley to serve.
8. **Variations & Ingredients Tips**:
9. Use veal scallopini instead of chicken for a classic piccata.
10. Add a splash of white wine to the sauce.
11. Serve over angel hair pasta or roasted vegetables.
12. **Per serving**: Calories: 310; Total Fat: 12g; Saturated Fat: 4g; Cholesterol: 105mg; Sodium: 630mg; Total Carbs: 14g; Dietary Fiber: 1g; Total Sugars: 2g; Protein: 33g

Cheesy Chicken Tenders

Servings: 4
Prep Time: 15 Minutes | Cooking Time: 25 Minutes
Ingredients:
- 1 cup grated Parmesan cheese
- ¼ cup grated cheddar
- 567 grams chicken tenders
- 1 egg, beaten
- 2 tbsp milk
- Salt and pepper to taste
- ½ tsp garlic powder
- 1 tsp dried thyme
- ¼ tsp shallot powder

Directions:
1. Preheat the air fryer to 200°C/400°F.
2. Stir the egg and milk until combined. Mix the salt, pepper, garlic, thyme, shallot, cheddar cheese, and Parmesan cheese on a plate.
3. Dip the chicken in the egg mix, then in the cheese mix, and press to coat.
4. Lay the tenders in the air fryer basket in a single layer. Add a raised rack to cook more at one time. Spray all with oil and Bake for 12-16 minutes, flipping once halfway through cooking.
5. Serve hot.
6. **Variations & Ingredients Tips:**
7. Use panko breadcrumbs or crushed cornflakes instead of cheese for a different crust.
8. Add a pinch of cayenne pepper or paprika to the coating for a spicy kick.
9. Serve with honey mustard, ranch, or marinara sauce for dipping.
10. **Per Serving**: Calories: 420; Total Fat: 21g; Saturated Fat: 9g; Sodium: 860mg; Total Carbohydrates: 4g; Dietary Fiber: 0g; Total Sugars: 1g; Protein: 51g

Nacho Chicken Fries

Servings: 4
Prep Time: 15 Minutes | Cooking Time: 7 Minutes
Ingredients:
- 450g chicken tenders
- Salt
- 1/4 cup flour
- 2 eggs
- 3/4 cup panko breadcrumbs
- 3/4 cup crushed organic nacho cheese tortilla chips
- Oil for misting or cooking spray
- Seasoning Mix:
- 1 tablespoon chili powder
- 1 teaspoon ground cumin
- 1/2 teaspoon garlic powder
- 1/2 teaspoon onion powder

Directions:
1. Stir together all seasonings in a small cup and set aside.
2. Cut chicken tenders in half crosswise, then cut into strips no wider than about 1.25 cm.
3. Preheat air fryer to 200°C/390°F.
4. Salt chicken to taste. Place strips in large bowl and sprinkle with 1 tablespoon of the seasoning mix. Stir well to distribute seasonings.
5. Add flour to chicken and stir well to coat all sides.
6. Beat eggs together in a shallow dish.
7. In a second shallow dish, combine the panko, crushed chips, and the remaining 2 teaspoons of seasoning mix.
8. Dip chicken strips in eggs, then roll in crumbs. Mist with oil or cooking spray.
9. Chicken strips will cook best if done in two batches. They can be crowded and overlapping a little but not stacked in double or triple layers.
10. Cook for 4 minutes. Shake basket, mist with oil, and cook 3 more minutes, until chicken juices run clear and outside is crispy.
11. Repeat step 10 to cook remaining chicken fries.
12. **Variations & Ingredients Tips:**
13. Use Cool Ranch Doritos or spicy nacho chips for different flavors.
14. Dip chicken fries in queso, guacamole or salsa.
15. Serve in tortillas with shredded lettuce, cheese and pico de gallo.
16. **Per serving**: Calories: 360; Total Fat: 14g; Saturated Fat: 3g; Cholesterol: 175mg; Sodium: 620mg; Total Carbs: 25g; Dietary Fiber: 2g; Total Sugars: 1g; Protein: 33g

Teriyaki Chicken Bites

Servings: 4
Prep Time: 15 Minutes | Cooking Time: 30 Minutes
Ingredients:
- 450g boneless, skinless chicken thighs, cubed
- 1 green onion, sliced diagonally

- 1 large egg
- 1 tbsp teriyaki sauce
- 4 tbsp flour
- 1 tsp sesame oil
- 2 tsp balsamic vinegar
- 2 tbsp tamari
- 3 cloves garlic, minced
- 2 tsp grated fresh ginger
- 2 tsp chili garlic sauce
- 2 tsp granular honey
- Salt and pepper to taste

Directions:
1. Preheat air fryer to 200°C/400°F.
2. Beat egg, teriyaki sauce and flour. Coat chicken pieces.
3. In another bowl, combine remaining ingredients except green onion.
4. Air fry chicken for 15 mins, tossing every 5 mins.
5. Toss cooked chicken in sauce.
6. Garnish with green onions.
7. **Variations & Ingredients Tips**:
8. Use chicken breasts instead of thighs.
9. Add broccoli, snap peas or water chestnuts.
10. Substitute honey for brown sugar or maple syrup.
11. **Per Serving**: Calories: 284; Total Fat: 11g; Saturated Fat: 2g; Cholesterol: 146mg; Sodium: 556mg; Total Carbs: 19g; Dietary Fiber: 1g; Total Sugars: 4g; Protein: 27g

Chicken Salad With Roasted Vegetables

Servings: 4
Prep Time: 10 Minutes | Cooking Time: 25 Minutes
Ingredients:
- 4 tbsp honey-mustard salad dressing
- 3 chicken breasts, cubed
- 1 red onion, sliced
- 1 orange bell pepper, sliced
- 1 cup sliced zucchini
- ½ tsp dried thyme
- ½ cup mayonnaise
- 2 tbsp lemon juice

Directions:
1. Preheat air fryer to 200°C/400°F.

2. Add chicken, onion, pepper, and zucchini to the fryer. Drizzle with 1 tbsp of the salad dressing and sprinkle with thyme. Toss to coat.
3. Bake for 5-6 minutes. Shake the basket, then continue cooking for another 5-6 minutes.
4. In a bowl, combine the rest of the dressing, mayonnaise, and lemon juice.
5. Transfer the chicken and vegetables and toss to coat.
6. Serve and enjoy!
7. **Variations & Ingredients Tips**:
8. Use a different dressing like ranch, Italian, or balsamic vinaigrette.
9. Add cherry tomatoes, mushrooms, or eggplant to the vegetable mix.
10. Serve over a bed of mixed greens or spinach for extra nutrients.
11. **Per Serving**: Calories: 420; Total Fat: 28g; Saturated Fat: 5g; Sodium: 420mg; Total Carbohydrates: 11g; Dietary Fiber: 2g; Total Sugars: 7g; Protein: 32g

Teriyaki Chicken Legs

Servings: 2
Prep Time: 5 Minutes | Cooking Time: 20 Minutes
Ingredients:
- 4 tablespoons teriyaki sauce
- 1 tablespoon orange juice
- 1 teaspoon smoked paprika
- 4 chicken legs
- Cooking spray

Directions:
1. Mix together teriyaki sauce, orange juice and smoked paprika.
2. Brush sauce mixture on all sides of chicken legs.
3. Spray air fryer basket with cooking spray and add chicken legs.
4. Cook at 180°C/360°F for 6 mins. Turn and baste with sauce.
5. Cook 6 more mins, turn and baste again.
6. Cook 8 additional mins until juices run clear when pierced.
7. **Variations & Ingredients Tips**:
8. Use chicken thighs or drumsticks instead of whole legs.
9. Add garlic powder, ginger or honey to the teriyaki sauce.

10. Brush with extra sauce after cooking and broil 2-3 mins for caramelization.

11. **Per Serving** (2 legs): Calories: 383; Total Fat: 18g; Saturated Fat: 4g; Cholesterol: 194mg; Sodium: 1096mg; Total Carbs: 15g; Dietary Fiber: 0g; Total Sugars: 10g; Protein: 41g

Masala Chicken With Charred Vegetables

Servings: 4

Prep Time: 15 Minutes (plus Marinating Time) | Cooking Time: 35 Minutes

Ingredients:

- 8 boneless, skinless chicken thighs
- 1/4 cup yogurt
- 3 garlic cloves, minced
- 1 tbsp lime juice
- 1 tsp ginger-garlic paste
- 1 tsp garam masala
- 1/4 tsp ground turmeric
- 1/4 tsp red pepper flakes
- 1 1/4 tsp salt
- 225g shishito peppers
- 2 vine tomatoes, quartered
- 1 tbsp chopped cilantro
- 1 lime, cut into wedges

Directions:

1. Mix yogurt, garlic, lime juice, ginger paste, garam masala, turmeric, flakes, and salt in a bowl. Place the thighs in a zipper bag and pour in the marinade. Massage the chicken to coat and refrigerate for 2 hours.

2. Preheat air fryer to 200°C/400°F. Remove the chicken from the bag and discard the marinade. Put the chicken in the greased frying basket and Air Fry for 13-15 minutes, flipping once until browned and thoroughly cooked. Set chicken aside and cover with foil.

3. Lightly spray shishitos and tomatoes with cooking oil. Place in the frying basket and Bake for 8 minutes, shaking the basket once until soft and slightly charred. Sprinkle with salt.

4. Top the chicken and veggies with cilantro and lemon wedges.

5. **Variations & Ingredients Tips**:

6. Substitute chicken with paneer, tofu or cauliflower for vegetarian options.

7. Add diced potatoes to the frying basket with the peppers.

8. Serve with naan bread and mint chutney.

9. **Per serving**: Calories: 300; Total Fat: 11g; Saturated Fat: 3g; Cholesterol: 185mg; Sodium: 850mg; Total Carbs: 8g; Dietary Fiber: 2g; Total Sugars: 4g; Protein: 41g

Cajun Chicken Livers

Servings: 2

Prep Time: 30 Minutes (plus 2 Hours Marinating Time) | Cooking Time: 45 Minutes

Ingredients:

- 454 grams chicken livers, rinsed, connective tissue discarded
- 1 cup whole milk
- ½ cup cornmeal
- 3/4 cup flour
- 1 tsp salt and black pepper
- 1 tsp Cajun seasoning
- 2 eggs
- 1 ½ cups bread crumbs
- 1 tbsp olive oil
- 2 tbsp chopped parsley

Directions:

1. Pat chicken livers dry with paper towels, then transfer them to a small bowl and pour in the milk and black pepper. Let sit covered in the fridge for 2 hours.

2. Preheat air fryer at 190°C/375°F.

3. In a bowl, combine cornmeal, flour, salt, and Cajun seasoning. In another bowl, beat the eggs, and in a third bowl, add bread crumbs.

4. Dip chicken livers first in the cornmeal mixture, then in the egg, and finally in the bread crumbs.

5. Place chicken livers in the greased air fryer basket, brush the tops lightly with olive oil, and Air Fry for 16 minutes, turning once.

6. Serve right away sprinkled with parsley.

7. **Variations & Ingredients Tips**:

8. Add a dash of hot sauce or cayenne pepper to the milk for extra spice.

9. Serve with a side of remoulade sauce, hot sauce, or ranch dressing for dipping.

10. Use a mixture of half cornmeal and half flour for a lighter coating.

11. **Per Serving**: Calories: 790; Total Fat: 30g; Saturated Fat: 9g; Sodium: 1530mg; Total

Carbohydrates: 73g; Dietary Fiber: 4g; Total Sugars: 9g; Protein: 61g

Berry-glazed Turkey Breast

Servings: 4
Prep Time: 15 Minutes | Cooking Time: 1 Hour 25 Minutes
Ingredients:
* 1 bone-in, skin-on turkey breast
* 1 tbsp olive oil
* Salt and pepper to taste
* 1 cup raspberries
* 1 cup chopped strawberries
* 2 tbsp balsamic vinegar
* 2 tbsp butter, melted
* 1 tbsp honey mustard
* 1 tsp dried rosemary

Directions:
1. Preheat the air fryer to 180°C/350°F.
2. Lay the turkey breast skin-side up in the air fryer basket, brush with the oil, and sprinkle with salt and pepper.
3. Bake for 55-65 minutes, flipping twice.
4. Meanwhile, mix the berries, vinegar, melted butter, rosemary and honey mustard in a blender and blend until smooth.
5. Turn the turkey skin-side up inside the fryer and brush with half of the berry mix. Bake for 5 more minutes.
6. Put the remaining berry mix in a small saucepan and simmer for 3-4 minutes while the turkey cooks.
7. When the turkey is done, let it stand for 10 minutes, then carve. Serve with the remaining glaze.
8. **Variations & Ingredients Tips**:
9. Use boneless, skinless turkey breast for quicker cooking time.
10. Substitute raspberries and strawberries with blackberries, blueberries, or cranberries.
11. Add a pinch of cayenne pepper or red pepper flakes to the glaze for a spicy kick.
12. **Per Serving**: Calories: 400; Total Fat: 15g; Saturated Fat: 5g; Sodium: 180mg; Total Carbohydrates: 14g; Dietary Fiber: 3g; Total Sugars: 10g; Protein: 52g

Yogurt-marinated Chicken Legs

Servings: 4
Prep Time: 10 Minutes (plus Marinating Time) | Cooking Time: 50 Minutes
Ingredients:
* 1 cup Greek yogurt
* 1 tbsp Dijon mustard
* 1 tsp smoked paprika
* 1 tbsp crushed red pepper
* 1 tsp garlic powder
* 1 tsp dried oregano
* 1 tsp dried thyme
* 1 teaspoon ground cumin
* 1/4 cup lemon juice
* Salt and pepper to taste
* 680g chicken legs
* 3 tbsp butter, melted

Directions:
1. Combine all ingredients, except chicken and butter, in a bowl. Fold in chicken legs and toss until coated. Let sit covered in the fridge for 60 minutes up to overnight.
2. Preheat air fryer at 190°C/375°F. Shake excess marinade from chicken; place them in the greased frying basket and Air Fry for 18 minutes, brush melted butter and flip once.
3. Let chill for 5 minutes before serving.
4. **Variations & Ingredients Tips**:
5. Use buttermilk or coconut milk instead of yogurt for a different flavor profile.
6. Add grated ginger or turmeric to the marinade for an Indian twist.
7. Serve with mint-cucumber raita or mango chutney on the side.
8. **Per serving**: Calories: 470; Total Fat: 30g; Saturated Fat: 12g; Cholesterol: 245mg; Sodium: 510mg; Total Carbs: 5g; Dietary Fiber: 1g; Total Sugars: 3g; Protein: 45g

Turkey & Rice Frittata

Servings: 4
Prep Time: 10 Minutes | Cooking Time: 30 Minutes
Ingredients:
* 6 large eggs
* 1/2 tsp dried thyme

- 1/2 cup rice, cooked
- 1/2 cup pulled turkey, cooked
- 1/2 cup fresh baby spinach
- 1 red bell pepper, chopped
- 2 tsp Parmesan cheese, grated

Directions:
1. Preheat air fryer to 160°C/320°F.
2. Put rice, turkey, spinach, and bell pepper in a greased pan.
3. Whisk eggs and thyme, then pour over rice mix.
4. Top with Parmesan and bake for 15 mins until puffed and golden.
5. Serve hot.
6. **Variations & Ingredients Tips**:
7. Use cooked chicken, ham or bacon instead of turkey.
8. Add onions, mushrooms or other cooked veggies.
9. Top with cheddar or feta cheese instead of parmesan.
10. **Per Serving**: Calories: 151; Total Fat: 6g; Saturated Fat: 2g; Cholesterol: 249mg; Sodium: 211mg; Total Carbs: 11g; Dietary Fiber: 1g; Total Sugars: 1g; Protein: 13g

Nashville Hot Chicken

Servings: 4
Prep Time: 20 Minutes | Cooking Time: 27 Minutes
Ingredients:
- 1 (1.8kg) chicken, cut into 6 pieces (2 breasts, 2 thighs and 2 drumsticks)
- 2 eggs
- 1 cup buttermilk
- 2 cups all-purpose flour
- 2 tablespoons paprika
- 1 teaspoon garlic powder
- 1 teaspoon onion powder
- 2 teaspoons salt
- 1 teaspoon freshly ground black pepper
- Vegetable oil, in a spray bottle
- Nashville Hot Sauce:
- 1 tablespoon cayenne pepper
- 1 teaspoon salt
- 1/4 cup vegetable oil
- 4 slices white bread
- Dill pickle slices

Directions:
1. Cut the chicken breasts into 2 pieces so that you have a total of 8 pieces of chicken.
2. Set up a two-stage dredging station. Whisk the eggs and buttermilk together in a bowl. Combine the flour, paprika, garlic powder, onion powder, salt and black pepper in a zipper-sealable plastic bag. Dip the chicken pieces into the egg-buttermilk mixture, then toss them in the seasoned flour, coating all sides. Repeat this procedure (egg mixture and then flour mixture) one more time. This can be a little messy, but make sure all sides of the chicken are completely covered. Spray the chicken with vegetable oil and set aside.
3. Preheat the air fryer to 190°C/370°F. Spray or brush the bottom of the air-fryer basket with a little vegetable oil.
4. Air-fry the chicken in two batches at 190°C/370°F for 20 minutes, flipping the pieces over halfway through the cooking process. Transfer the chicken to a plate, but do not cover. Repeat with the second batch of chicken.
5. Lower the temperature on the air fryer to 170°C/340°F. Flip the chicken back over and place the first batch of chicken on top of the second batch already in the basket. Air-fry for another 7 minutes.
6. While the chicken is air-frying, combine the cayenne pepper and salt in a bowl. Heat the vegetable oil in a small saucepan and when it is very hot, add it to the spice mix, whisking until smooth. It will sizzle briefly when you add it to the spices.
7. Place the fried chicken on top of the white bread slices and brush the hot sauce all over chicken. Top with the pickle slices and serve warm. Enjoy the heat and the flavor!
8. **Variations & Ingredients Tips**:
9. Adjust the cayenne to your spice preference.
10. Use chicken tenders for easier prep and cooking.
11. Serve in a sandwich with coleslaw and comeback sauce.
12. **Per serving**: Calories: 860; Total Fat: 58g; Saturated Fat: 12g; Cholesterol: 290mg; Sodium: 2210mg; Total Carbs: 36g; Dietary Fiber: 2g; Total Sugars: 5g; Protein: 55g

Smoky Chicken Fajita Bowl

Servings:4
Prep Time: 10 Minutes (plus 30 Minutes Chilling Time) | Cooking Time: 35 Minutes + Chilling Time
Ingredients:

- 1 jalapeño, sliced and seeded
- ½ cup queso fresco crumbles
- 1 tbsp olive oil
- 2 tsp flour
- ¼ tsp chili powder
- ¼ tsp fajita seasoning
- ¼ tsp smoked paprika
- ¼ tsp ground cumin
- ½ tsp granular honey
- ⅛ tsp onion powder
- ⅛ tsp garlic powder
- 454 grams chicken breast strips
- 4 tomatoes, diced
- ½ diced red onion
- 4 tbsp sour cream
- 1 avocado, diced

Directions:

1. Combine the olive oil, flour, all the spices, and chicken strips in a bowl. Let chill in the fridge for 30 minutes.
2. Preheat air fryer to 200°C/400°F.
3. Place the chicken strips in the air fryer basket and Air Fry for 8 minutes, shaking once.
4. Divide between 4 medium bowls. Add tomatoes, jalapeño, onion, queso fresco, sour cream, and avocado to the bowls.
5. Serve right away.
6. **Variations & Ingredients Tips**:
7. Use boneless, skinless chicken thighs instead of breasts for juicier meat.
8. Add sliced bell peppers, corn, or black beans to the bowls for extra veggies and fiber.
9. Serve with a side of salsa, guacamole, or tortilla chips for dipping.
10. **Per Serving**: Calories: 400; Total Fat: 23g; Saturated Fat: 7g; Sodium: 390mg; Total

Carbohydrates: 15g; Dietary Fiber: 5g; Total Sugars: 6g; Protein: 37g

Sunday Chicken Skewers

Servings: 4
Prep Time: 15 Minutes | Cooking Time: 25 Minutes
Ingredients:
- 1 green bell pepper, cut into chunks
- 1 red bell pepper, cut into chunks
- 4 chicken breasts, cubed
- 1 tbsp chicken seasoning
- Salt and pepper to taste
- 16 cherry tomatoes
- 8 pearl onions, peeled

Directions:

1. Preheat air fryer to 180°C/360°F.
2. Season the chicken cubes with chicken seasoning, salt, and pepper.
3. Thread metal skewers with chicken, bell pepper chunks, cherry tomatoes, and pearl onions.
4. Put the kabobs in the greased frying basket.
5. Bake for 14-16 minutes, flipping once until cooked through.
6. Let cool slightly. Serve.
7. **Variations & Ingredients Tips**:
8. Use boneless, skinless chicken thighs for more flavor.
9. Marinate the chicken in Italian dressing before threading.
10. Add mushrooms, zucchini or pineapple chunks to the skewers.
11. **Per Serving** (2 skewers): Calories: 259; Total Fat: 4g; Saturated Fat: 1g; Cholesterol: 83mg; Sodium: 352mg; Total Carbs: 18g; Dietary Fiber: 3g; Total Sugars: 8g; Protein: 38g

Beef, Pork & Lamb Recipes

Mushroom & Quinoa-stuffed Pork Loins

Servings: 3
Prep Time: 20 Minutes | Cooking Time: 25 Minutes
Ingredients:
- 3 boneless center-cut pork loins, pocket cut in each loin
- ½ cup diced white mushrooms
- 1 teaspoon vegetable oil
- 3 bacon slices, diced
- ½ onion, peeled and diced
- 1 cup baby spinach
- Salt and pepper to taste
- ½ cup cooked quinoa
- ½ cup mozzarella cheese

Directions:
1. Warm the oil in a skillet over medium heat. Add the bacon and cook for 3 minutes until the fat is rendered but not crispy. Add in onion and mushrooms and stir-fry for 3 minutes until the onions are translucent. Stir in spinach, salt, and pepper and cook for 1 minute until the spinach wilts. Set aside and toss in quinoa.
2. Preheat air fryer at 180°C/350°F. Stuff quinoa mixture into each pork loin and sprinkle with mozzarella cheese. Place them in the frying basket and Air Fry for 11 minutes.
3. Let rest onto a cutting board for 5 minutes before serving.
4. **Variations & Ingredients Tips**:
5. Use different types of mushrooms, such as shiitake or portobello, for a variety of flavors and textures.
6. Add some chopped nuts, such as walnuts or pecans, to the quinoa mixture for a crunchy texture.
7. Serve the stuffed pork loins with a side of roasted vegetables or a salad for a complete meal.
8. **Per Serving**: Calories: 430; Total Fat: 24g; Saturated Fat: 9g; Cholesterol: 115mg; Sodium: 470mg; Total Carbs: 8g; Fiber: 1g; Sugars: 1g; Protein: 45g

Corned Beef Hash

Servings: 6

Prep Time: 10 Minutes | Cooking Time: 15 Minutes
Ingredients:
- 3 cups (about 400 g) frozen unseasoned hash brown cubes (no need to thaw)
- 255 g deli corned beef, cut into 2 cm thick slices, then cubed
- ¾ cup roughly chopped yellow or white onion
- ¾ cup stemmed, cored, and roughly chopped red bell pepper
- 2½ tablespoons olive oil
- ¼ teaspoon dried thyme
- ¼ teaspoon dried sage leaves
- Up to a ⅛ teaspoon cayenne

Directions:
1. Preheat the air fryer to 200°C/400°F.
2. Mix all the ingredients in a large or very large bowl until the potato cubes and corned beef are coated in the spices.
3. Spread the mixture in the basket in as close to an even layer as you can. Air-fry for 15 minutes, tossing and rearranging the pieces at the 5- and 10-minute marks to expose covered bits, until the potatoes are browned, even crisp, and the mixture is very fragrant.
4. Pour the contents of the basket onto a serving platter or divide between serving plates. Cool for a couple of minutes before serving.
5. **Variations & Ingredients Tips**:
6. Use different types of potatoes, such as sweet potatoes or russet potatoes, for a variety of flavors and textures.
7. Add some minced garlic or jalapeño peppers for extra flavor and heat.
8. Top the corned beef hash with a fried egg for a classic breakfast dish.
9. **Per Serving**: Calories: 220; Total Fat: 12g; Saturated Fat: 3.5g; Cholesterol: 40mg; Sodium: 480mg; Total Carbs: 17g; Fiber: 1g; Sugars: 1g; Protein: 11g

Indian Fry Bread Tacos

Servings: 4
Prep Time: 15 Minutes | Cooking Time: 20 Minutes
Ingredients:

- 1 cup all-purpose flour
- 1½ tsp salt, divided
- 1½ tsp baking powder
- ¼ cup milk
- ¼ cup warm water
- 227 g lean ground beef
- One 410g can pinto beans, drained and rinsed
- 1 tbsp taco seasoning
- ½ cup shredded cheddar cheese
- 2 cups shredded lettuce
- ¼ cup black olives, chopped
- 1 Roma tomato, diced
- 1 avocado, diced
- 1 lime

Directions:

1. In a large bowl, whisk together the flour, 1 tsp of the salt, and baking powder. Make a well in the center and add in the milk and water. Form a ball and gently knead the dough four times. Cover the bowl with a damp towel, and set aside.

2. Preheat the air fryer to 190°C/380°F.

3. In a medium bowl, mix together the ground beef, beans, and taco seasoning. Crumble the meat mixture into the air fryer basket and cook for 5 minutes; toss the meat and cook an additional 2 to 3 minutes, or until cooked fully. Place the cooked meat in a bowl for taco assembly; season with the remaining ½ tsp salt as desired.

4. On a floured surface, place the dough. Cut the dough into 4 equal parts. Using a rolling pin, roll out each piece of dough to 12.5 cm in diameter. Spray the dough with cooking spray and place in the air fryer basket, working in batches as needed. Cook for 3 minutes, flip over, spray with cooking spray, and cook for an additional 1 to 3 minutes, until golden and puffy.

5. To assemble, place the fry breads on a serving platter. Equally divide the meat and bean mixture on top of the fry bread. Divide the cheese, lettuce, olives, tomatoes, and avocado among the four tacos. Squeeze lime over the top prior to serving.

6. **Variations & Ingredients Tips:**

7. Use ground turkey or shredded chicken instead of beef

8. Add some sliced jalapeños or hot sauce for a spicy kick

9. Offer sour cream, salsa and cilantro as additional toppings

10. **Per Serving**: Calories: 621; Total Fat: 28g; Saturated Fat: 9g; Cholesterol: 62mg; Sodium: 1472mg; Total Carbs: 64g; Dietary Fiber: 11g; Total Sugars: 3g; Protein: 30g

Lamb Burger With Feta And Olives

Servings: 3
Prep Time: 10 Minutes | Cooking Time: 16 Minutes
Ingredients:
- 2 teaspoons olive oil
- 1/3 onion, finely chopped
- 1 clove garlic, minced
- 450g ground lamb
- 2 tablespoons fresh parsley, finely chopped
- 1.5 teaspoons fresh oregano, finely chopped
- 1/2 cup black olives, finely chopped
- 1/3 cup crumbled feta cheese
- 1/2 teaspoon salt
- Freshly ground black pepper
- 4 thick pita breads
- Toppings and condiments

Directions:

1. Preheat a medium skillet over medium-high heat. Add the olive oil and cook the onion until tender, but not browned, about 4-5 minutes. Add the garlic and cook for 1 more minute.

2. Transfer the onion and garlic to a mixing bowl. Add the ground lamb, parsley, oregano, olives, feta cheese, salt, and pepper. Gently mix the ingredients together.

3. Divide the mixture into 3 or 4 equal portions and form into patties, making an indentation in the center of each.

4. Preheat the air fryer to 187°C/370°F.

5. Cook the burgers in batches - 2 or 3 at a time - for 8 minutes. Flip and cook for another 8 minutes. If cooking in batches, return the first batch to the air fryer for the last 2 minutes to reheat.

6. Remove the burgers to a resting plate and let them rest for a few minutes.

7. While the burgers rest, toast the pita breads in the air fryer for 2 minutes.

8. Tuck the burgers into the toasted pita breads or wrap the pitas around the burgers. Serve with desired toppings and condiments.

9. **Variations & Ingredients Tips:**

10. Sanjo Variation: For a Sanjo-style twist, add 1 teaspoon of ground cumin and 1/4 teaspoon of ground cinnamon to the burger mixture. The warm Middle Eastern spices complement the lamb, feta and olives.

11. Swap out the black olives for kalamata olives or a mix of olives for more briny flavor.

12. Serve the burgers on toasted brioche buns instead of pita for a richer, more indulgent base.

13. **Per Serving**: Calories: 456; Total Fat: 28g; Saturated Fat: 11g; Cholesterol: 112mg; Sodium: 701mg; Total Carbs: 24g; Dietary Fiber: 3g; Total Sugars: 2g; Protein: 29g

Ground Beef Calzones

Servings: 6
Prep Time: 20 Minutes | Cooking Time: 30 Minutes
Ingredients:
- 1 refrigerated pizza dough
- 1 cup shredded mozzarella
- ½ cup chopped onion
- 2 garlic cloves, minced
- ¼ cup chopped mushrooms
- 454 g ground beef
- 1 tbsp pizza seasoning
- Salt and pepper to taste
- 355 g marinara sauce
- 1 tsp flour

Directions:
1. Warm 1 tbsp of oil in a skillet over medium heat. Stir-fry onion, garlic and mushrooms for 2-3 minutes or until aromatic. Add beef, pizza seasoning, salt and pepper. Use a large spoon to break up the beef. Cook for 3 minutes or until brown. Stir in marinara sauce and set aside.

2. On a floured work surface, roll out pizza dough and cut into 6 equal-sized rectangles. On each rectangle, add ½ cup of beef and top with 1 tbsp of shredded cheese. Fold one side of the dough over the filling to the opposite side. Press the edges using the back of a fork to seal them. Preheat air fryer to 200°C/400°F. Place the first batch of calzones in the air fryer and spray with cooking oil. Bake for 10 minutes. Let cool slightly and serve warm.

3. **Variations & Ingredients Tips**:
4. Use Italian sausage instead of ground beef for a spicier flavor
5. Add some chopped pepperoni or ham to the filling

6. Brush the calzones with garlic butter before air frying for extra richness

7. **Per Serving**: Calories: 481; Total Fat: 21g; Saturated Fat: 8g; Cholesterol: 77mg; Sodium: 912mg; Total Carbs: 44g; Dietary Fiber: 3g; Total Sugars: 6g; Protein: 30g

Teriyaki Country-style Pork Ribs

Servings: 3
Prep Time: 10 Minutes | Cooking Time: 30 Minutes
Ingredients:
- 3 tablespoons Regular or low-sodium soy sauce or gluten-free tamari sauce
- 3 tablespoons Honey
- 3/4 teaspoon Ground dried ginger
- 3/4 teaspoon Garlic powder
- 3 227g boneless country-style pork ribs
- Vegetable oil spray

Directions:
1. Preheat the air fryer to 350°F/177°C.
2. Mix the soy or tamari sauce, honey, ground ginger, and garlic powder in another bowl until uniform.
3. Smear about half of this teriyaki sauce over all sides of the country-style ribs. Reserve the remainder of the teriyaki sauce. Generously coat the meat with vegetable oil spray.
4. When the machine is at temperature, place the country-style ribs in the basket with as much air space between them as possible. Air-fry undisturbed for 15 minutes. Turn the country-style ribs (but keep the space between them) and brush them all over with the remaining teriyaki sauce. Continue air-frying undisturbed for 15 minutes, or until an instant-read meat thermometer inserted into the center of one rib registers at least 145°F/63°C.
5. Use kitchen tongs to transfer the country-style ribs to a wire rack. Cool for 5 minutes before serving.
6. **Variations & Ingredients Tips**:
7. Use boneless pork loin or tenderloin instead of country-style ribs
8. Add crushed red pepper or sriracha to the teriyaki sauce for extra heat
9. Sprinkle with sesame seeds or sliced green onions before serving
10. **Per Serving**: Calories: 525; Total Fat: 24g; Saturated Fat: 8g; Cholesterol: 155mg; Sodium: 790mg;

Total Carbs: 30g; Dietary Fiber: 0g; Total Sugars: 24g; Protein: 44g

Country-style Pork Ribs(1)

Servings: 4
Prep Time: 10 Minutes | Cooking Time: 30 Minutes
Ingredients:

- 2 tablespoons cornstarch
- 2 tablespoons olive oil
- 1 teaspoon mustard powder
- ½ teaspoon thyme
- ½ teaspoon garlic powder
- 1 teaspoon paprika
- Salt and pepper to taste
- 12 country-style pork ribs

Directions:

1. Preheat air fryer to 200°C/400°F.
2. Mix together cornstarch, olive oil, mustard powder, thyme, garlic powder, paprika, salt, and pepper in a bowl.
3. Rub the seasoned mixture onto the ribs.
4. Put the ribs into the frying basket.
5. Bake for 14-16 minutes, flipping once until the ribs are crisp.
6. Serve.
7. **Variations & Ingredients Tips**:
8. Use different types of seasoning, such as barbecue rub or Cajun seasoning, for a variety of flavors.
9. Brush the ribs with your favorite barbecue sauce during the last few minutes of cooking for a sticky glaze.
10. Serve the pork ribs with a side of coleslaw or baked beans for a classic barbecue meal.
11. **Per Serving**: Calories: 510; Total Fat: 38g; Saturated Fat: 12g; Cholesterol: 140mg; Sodium: 180mg; Total Carbs: 5g; Fiber: 0g; Sugars: 0g; Protein: 36g

Cajun Pork Loin Chops

Servings: 4
Prep Time: 20 Minutes | Cooking Time: 25 Minutes
Ingredients:

- 8 thin boneless pork loin chops (около 680g total)
- 3.75ml Coarse sea salt
- 1 egg, beaten
- 5ml Cajun seasoning

- 120g bread crumbs
- 1 cucumber, sliced
- 1 tomato, sliced

Directions:

1. Place the chops between two sheets of parchment paper. Pound the pork to 6mm thickness using a meat mallet or rolling pin. Season with sea salt. In a shallow bowl, beat the egg with 5ml of water and Cajun seasoning. In a second bowl, add the breadcrumbs. Dip the chops into the egg mixture, shake, and dip into the crumbs.
2. Preheat air fryer to 400°F/205°C. Place the chops in the greased frying basket and Air Fry for 6-8 minutes, flipping once until golden and cooked through. Serve immediately with cucumber and tomato.
3. **Variations & Ingredients Tips**:
4. Use panko breadcrumbs instead of regular for an extra crispy coating
5. Make a remoulade or comeback sauce for dipping
6. Let the breaded chops rest for 10 minutes before frying for a better crust
7. **Per Serving**: Calories 250; Total Fat 8g; Saturated Fat 2.5g; Cholesterol 135mg; Sodium 540mg; Total Carbs 15g; Fiber 1g; Sugars 1g; Protein 29g

German-style Pork Patties

Servings: 6
Prep Time: 10 Minutes | Cooking Time: 35 Minutes
Ingredients:

- 450g ground pork
- ¼ cup diced fresh pear
- 1 tbsp minced sage leaves
- 1 garlic clove, minced
- 2 tbsp chopped chives
- Salt and pepper to taste

Directions:

1. Preheat the air fryer to 190°C/375°F. Combine the pork, pear, sage, chives, garlic, salt, and pepper in a bowl and mix gently but thoroughly with your hands, then make 8 patties about 3 cm thick. Lay the patties in the frying basket in a single layer and Air Fry for 15-20 minutes, flipping once halfway through. Remove and drain on paper towels, then serve. Serve and enjoy!
2. **Variations & Ingredients Tips**:
3. Mix in some shredded apple for extra sweetness and moisture

4. Serve on pretzel buns with grainy mustard and sauerkraut

5. Form the patties around cubes of Swiss cheese for a melty surprise

6. **Per Serving**: Calories: 227; Total Fat: 17g; Saturated Fat: 6g; Cholesterol: 65mg; Sodium: 80mg; Total Carbs: 2g; Dietary Fiber: 0g; Total Sugars: 1g; Protein: 16g

Kentucky-style Pork Tenderloin

Servings: 2
Prep Time: 10 Minutes | Cooking Time: 30 Minutes
Ingredients:

- 454g pork tenderloin, halved crosswise
- 1 tbsp smoked paprika
- 2 tsp ground cumin
- 1 tsp garlic powder
- 1 tsp shallot powder
- 1/4 tsp chili pepper
- Salt and pepper to taste
- 1 tsp Italian seasoning
- 2 tbsp butter, melted
- 1 tsp Worcestershire sauce

Directions:

1. Preheat air fryer to 350°F/177°C. In a shallow bowl, combine all spices. Set aside. In another bowl, whisk butter and Worcestershire sauce and brush over pork tenderloin. Sprinkle with the seasoning mix. Place pork in the lightly greased frying basket and Air Fry for 16 minutes, flipping once. Let sit onto a cutting board for 5 minutes before slicing. Serve immediately.

2. **Variations & Ingredients Tips**:

3. Use smoked paprika or chipotle powder for a smoky flavor

4. Add brown sugar or honey to the spice rub for a sweet-spicy glaze

5. Brush tenderloin with mustard before applying rub for extra tang

6. **Per serving**: Calories: 375; Total Fat: 16g; Saturated Fat: 7g; Cholesterol: 145mg; Sodium: 580mg; Total Carbs: 7g; Dietary Fiber: 2g; Total Sugars: 2g; Protein: 48g

Brie And Cranberry Burgers

Servings: 3
Prep Time: 15 Minutes | Cooking Time: 9 Minutes
Ingredients:

- 454g ground beef (80% lean)
- 1 tablespoon chopped fresh thyme
- 1 tablespoon Worcestershire sauce
- 1/2 teaspoon salt
- Freshly ground black pepper
- 1 (113g) wheel of Brie cheese, sliced
- Handful of arugula
- 3 or 4 brioche hamburger buns (or potato hamburger buns), toasted
- 57-114g whole berry cranberry sauce

Directions:

1. Combine the beef, thyme, Worcestershire sauce, salt and pepper together in a large bowl and mix well. Divide the meat into 4 (113g) portions or 3 larger portions and then form them into burger patties, being careful not to over-handle the meat.

2. Preheat the air fryer to 390°F/200°C and pour a little water into the bottom of the air fryer drawer. (This will help prevent the grease that drips into the bottom drawer from burning and smoking.)

3. Transfer the burgers to the air fryer basket. Air-fry the burgers at 390°F/200°C for 5 minutes. Flip the burgers over and air-fry for another 2 minutes. Top each burger with a couple slices of brie and air-fry for another minute or two, just to soften the cheese.

4. Build the burgers by placing a few leaves of arugula on the bottom bun, adding the burger and a spoonful of cranberry sauce on top. Top with the other half of the hamburger bun and enjoy.

5. **Variations & Ingredients Tips**:

6. Use goat cheese or camembert instead of brie for a different flavor

7. Add caramelized onions on top for extra flavor

8. Brush the buns with garlic butter before toasting

9. **Per Serving**: Calories 620; Total Fat 32g; Saturated Fat 14g; Cholesterol 120mg; Sodium 870mg; Total Carbs 42g; Fiber 2g; Sugars 11g; Protein 38g

Bourbon Bacon Burgers

Servings: 2
Prep Time: 15 Minutes | Cooking Time: 23 Minutes
Ingredients:

- 1 tablespoon bourbon

- 2 tablespoons brown sugar
- 3 strips maple bacon, cut into 7.5 cm pieces
- 340g ground beef (80% lean)
- 1 tablespoon minced onion
- 2 tablespoons BBQ sauce
- 2.5 ml salt
- Freshly ground black pepper
- 2 slices Colby Jack cheese (or Monterey Jack)
- 2 kaiser rolls
- Lettuce and tomato, for serving
- Zesty Burger Sauce:
- 2 tablespoons BBQ sauce
- 2 tablespoons mayonnaise
- 1.25 ml ground paprika
- Freshly ground black pepper

Directions:

1. Preheat the air fryer to 200°C/390°F and pour a little water into the bottom of the air fryer drawer. (This will help prevent the grease that drips into the bottom drawer from burning and smoking.)

2. Combine the bourbon and brown sugar in a small bowl. Place the bacon strips in the air fryer basket and brush with the brown sugar mixture. Air-fry at 200°C/390°F for 4 minutes. Flip the bacon over, brush with more brown sugar and air-fry at 200°C/390°F for an additional 4 minutes until crispy.

3. While the bacon is cooking, make the burger patties. Combine the ground beef, onion, BBQ sauce, salt and pepper in a large bowl. Mix together thoroughly with your hands and shape the meat into 2 patties.

4. Transfer the burger patties to the air fryer basket and air-fry the burgers at 190°C/370°F for 15 to 20 minutes, depending on how you like your burger cooked (15 minutes for rare to medium-rare; 20 minutes for well-done). Flip the burgers over halfway through the cooking process.

5. While the burgers are air-frying, make the burger sauce by combining the BBQ sauce, mayonnaise, paprika and freshly ground black pepper in a bowl.

6. When the burgers are cooked to your liking, top each patty with a slice of Colby Jack cheese and air-fry for an additional minute, just to melt the cheese. (You might want to pin the cheese slice to the burger with a toothpick to prevent it from blowing off in your air fryer.)

7. Spread the sauce on the inside of the Kaiser rolls, place the burgers on the rolls, top with the bourbon bacon, lettuce and tomato and enjoy!

8. **Variations & Ingredients Tips**:

9. For a smokier flavor, use smoked paprika instead of regular paprika in the zesty burger sauce.

10. Add some crumbled blue cheese or gorgonzola to the burger patties for a tangy kick.

11. Use brioche buns instead of Kaiser rolls for an extra buttery, rich burger bun.

12. **Per Serving**:

13. Calories 798; Total Fat 48g; Saturated Fat 17g; Cholesterol 151mg; Sodium 1442mg; Total Carbs 50g; Fiber 2g; Sugars 22g; Protein 41g

Skirt Steak With Horseradish Cream

Servings: 2
Prep Time: 10 Minutes | Cooking Time: 20 Minutes
Ingredients:
- 1 cup heavy cream
- 3 tablespoons horseradish sauce
- 1 lemon, zested
- 1 skirt steak, halved
- 2 tablespoons olive oil
- Salt and pepper to taste

Directions:

1. Mix together the heavy cream, horseradish sauce, and lemon zest in a small bowl. Let chill in the fridge.

2. Preheat air fryer to 200°C/400°F. Brush steak halves with olive oil and sprinkle with salt and pepper. Place steaks in the frying basket and Air Fry for 10 minutes or until you reach your desired doneness, flipping once. Let sit onto a cutting board for 5 minutes. Thinly slice against the grain and divide between 2 plates. Drizzle with the horseradish sauce over. Serve and enjoy!

3. **Variations & Ingredients Tips**:

4. Use sour cream or crème fraîche instead of heavy cream for a tangy twist

5. Add some chopped chives or parsley to the sauce for freshness

6. Serve with roasted potatoes, grilled asparagus or a simple salad

7. **Per Serving**: Calories: 738; Total Fat: 67g; Saturated Fat: 33g; Cholesterol: 174mg; Sodium:

262mg; Total Carbs: 7g; Dietary Fiber: 1g; Total Sugars: 4g; Protein: 31g

Peachy Pork Chops

Servings: 2
Prep Time: 35 Minutes | Cooking Time: 20 Minutes
Ingredients:
- 2 tablespoons peach preserves
- 2 tablespoons tomato paste
- 1 tablespoon Dijon mustard
- 1 teaspoon BBQ sauce
- 1 tablespoon lime juice
- 1 tablespoon olive oil
- 2 cloves garlic, minced
- 2 pork chops

Directions:
1. Whisk all ingredients in a bowl until well mixed and let chill covered in the fridge for 30 minutes.
2. Preheat air fryer to 180°C/350°F. Place pork chops in the frying basket and Air Fry for 12 minutes or until cooked through and tender.
3. Transfer the chops to a cutting board and let sit for 5 minutes before serving.
4. **Variations & Ingredients Tips**:
5. Use different types of fruit preserves, such as apricot or mango, for a variety of flavors.
6. Add some chopped fresh herbs, such as thyme or rosemary, to the marinade for extra flavor.
7. Serve the pork chops with a side of grilled peaches or a peach salsa for a fruity twist.
8. **Per Serving**: Calories: 320; Total Fat: 16g; Saturated Fat: 4g; Cholesterol: 90mg; Sodium: 520mg; Total Carbs: 16g; Fiber: 1g; Sugars: 12g; Protein: 29g

Honey Pork Links

Servings: 4
Prep Time: 10 Minutes | Cooking Time: 20 Minutes
Ingredients:
- 340 g ground mild pork sausage, removed from casings
- 1 tsp rubbed sage
- 2 tbsp honey
- ⅛ tsp cayenne pepper
- ⅛ tsp paprika
- Salt and pepper to taste

Directions:
1. Preheat air fryer to 200°C/400°F. Remove the sausage from the casings. Transfer to a bowl and add the remaining ingredients. Mix well. Make 8 links out of the mixture. Add the links to the frying basket and Air Fry for 8-10 minutes, flipping once. Serve right away.
2. **Variations & Ingredients Tips**:
3. Use hot Italian sausage for a spicier kick
4. Brush the links with BBQ sauce in the last few minutes of cooking
5. Serve in hot dog buns with sautéed peppers and onions
6. **Per Serving**: Calories: 309; Total Fat: 23g; Saturated Fat: 8g; Cholesterol: 71mg; Sodium: 571mg; Total Carbs: 9g; Dietary Fiber: 0g; Total Sugars: 9g; Protein: 17g

Traditional Moo Shu Pork Lettuce Wraps

Servings: 4
Prep Time: 15 Minutes | Cooking Time: 40 Minutes
Ingredients:
- 1/2 cup sliced shiitake mushrooms
- 454g boneless pork loin, cubed
- 3 tbsp cornstarch
- 2 tbsp rice vinegar
- 3 tbsp hoisin sauce
- 1 tsp oyster sauce
- 3 tsp sesame oil
- 1 tsp sesame seeds
- 1/4 tsp ground ginger
- 1 egg
- 2 tbsp flour
- 1 bag coleslaw mix
- 1 cup chopped baby spinach
- 3 green onions, sliced
- 8 iceberg lettuce leaves

Directions:
1. Preheat air fryer at 350°F/177°C. Make a slurry by whisking 1 tbsp of cornstarch and 1 tbsp of water in a bowl. Set aside. Warm a saucepan over heat, add in rice vinegar, hoisin sauce, oyster sauce, 1 tsp of sesame oil, and ginger, and cook for 3 minutes, stirring often. Add in cornstarch slurry and cook for 1 minute. Set aside

and let the mixture thicken. Beat the egg, flour, and the remaining cornstarch in a bowl. Set aside.

2. Dredge pork cubes in the egg mixture. Shake off any excess. Place them in the greased frying basket and Air Fry for 8 minutes, shaking once. Warm the remaining sesame oil in a skillet over medium heat. Add in coleslaw mix, baby spinach, green onions, and mushrooms and cook for 5 minutes until the coleslaw wilts. Turn the heat off. Add in cooked pork, pour in oyster sauce mixture, and toss until coated. Divide mixture between lettuce leaves, sprinkle with sesame seed, roll them up, and serve.

3. **Variations & Ingredients Tips**:

4. Use ground pork instead of pork loin for easier preparation

5. Add shredded carrots or bean sprouts to the filling

6. Substitute rice vinegar with balsamic or red wine vinegar

7. **Per Serving**: Calories: 385; Total Fat: 12g; Saturated Fat: 3g; Cholesterol: 95mg; Sodium: 740mg; Total Carbs: 45g; Dietary Fiber: 6g; Total Sugars: 12g; Protein: 26g

Beefy Quesadillas

Servings: 4
Prep Time: 15 Minutes | Cooking Time: 45 Minutes
Ingredients:

- 2 cups grated cheddar
- 1 tsp chili powder
- ½ tsp smoked paprika
- ½ tsp ground cumin
- ½ tsp nutmeg
- ¼ tsp garlic powder
- Salt and pepper to taste
- 1 ribeye steak
- 2 tsp olive oil
- 1 red bell pepper, diced
- 1 grated carrot
- 1 green bell pepper, diced
- ½ red onion, sliced
- 1 cup corn kernels
- 3 tbsp butter, melted
- 8 tortillas

Directions:

1. Mix the chili powder, nutmeg, paprika, cumin, garlic powder, salt, and pepper in a bowl. Toss in ribeye until fully coated and let marinate covered in the

fridge for 30 minutes. Preheat air fryer at 200°C/400°F. Place ribeye in the greased frying basket and bake for 6 minutes until rare, flipping once. Let rest onto a cutting board for 5 minutes before slicing thinly against the grain. Warm the olive oil in a skillet over high heat. Add in bell peppers, carrot and onion and cook for 6-8 minutes until the peppers are tender. Stir in corn. Set aside. Preheat air fryer at 175°C/350°F. Brush on one side of a tortilla lightly with melted butter. Layer ¼ beef strips, ¼ bell pepper mixture, and finally, ¼ of the grated cheese. Top with a second tortilla and lightly brush with butter on top. Repeat with the remaining ingredients. Place quesadillas, butter side down, in the frying basket and bake for 3 minutes. Cut them into 6 sections and serve.

2. **Variations & Ingredients Tips**:

3. Use chicken, pork, or shrimp instead of beef for different protein options.

4. Add sliced jalapeños, black beans, or diced tomatoes to the veggie mixture for extra flavor.

5. Serve with salsa, guacamole, or sour cream for dipping.

6. **Per Serving**: Calories: 679; Total Fat: 44g; Saturated Fat: 22g; Cholesterol: 134mg; Sodium: 727mg; Total Carbohydrates: 40g; Dietary Fiber: 5g; Total Sugars: 6g; Protein: 33g

Stuffed Pork Chops

Servings: 4
Prep Time: 10 Minutes | Cooking Time: 12 Minutes
Ingredients:

- 4 boneless pork chops
- ½ teaspoon salt
- ½ teaspoon black pepper
- ¼ teaspoon paprika
- 1 cup frozen spinach, defrosted and squeezed dry
- 2 cloves garlic, minced
- 57 g cream cheese
- 28 g grated Parmesan cheese
- 1 tablespoon extra-virgin olive oil

Directions:

1. Pat the pork chops with a paper towel. Make a slit in the side of each pork chop to create a pouch.

2. Season the pork chops with the salt, pepper, and paprika.

3. In a small bowl, mix together the spinach, garlic, cream cheese, and Parmesan cheese.

4. Divide the mixture into fourths and stuff the pork chop pouches. Secure the pouches with toothpicks.

5. Preheat the air fryer to 200°C/400°F.

6. Place the stuffed pork chops in the air fryer basket and spray liberally with cooking spray. Cook for 6 minutes, flip and coat with more cooking spray, and cook another 6 minutes. Check to make sure the meat is cooked to an internal temperature of 63°C/145°F. Cook the pork chops in batches, as needed.

7. **Variations & Ingredients Tips**:

8. Use kale, chard or arugula instead of spinach

9. Add some diced sun-dried tomatoes or roasted red peppers to the filling

10. Wrap the stuffed chops with prosciutto or bacon before air frying

11. **Per Serving**: Calories: 288; Total Fat: 17g; Saturated Fat: 7g; Cholesterol: 100mg; Sodium: 521mg; Total Carbs: 3g; Dietary Fiber: 1g; Total Sugars: 1g; Protein: 32g

Balsamic Marinated Rib Eye Steak With Balsamic Fried Cipollini Onions

Servings: 2
Prep Time: 10 Minutes (plus Marinating Time) | Cooking Time: 22-26 Minutes
Ingredients:

- 3 tablespoons balsamic vinegar, divided
- 2 garlic cloves, sliced
- 1 tablespoon Dijon mustard
- 1 teaspoon fresh thyme leaves
- 1 (400g) boneless rib eye steak
- Coarsely ground black pepper
- Salt
- 227g bag cipollini onions, peeled

Directions:

1. Combine 3 tbsp vinegar, garlic, mustard and thyme. Pour over steak and pierce with a fork. Season generously with pepper.

2. Marinate steak 2-24 hours in the fridge. Let sit at room temp 30 mins before cooking.

3. Preheat air fryer to 204°C/400°F.

4. Season steak with salt and air fry for 12-16 mins, flipping halfway, until desired doneness.

5. Toss onions with 1 tsp vinegar and salt.

6. Remove steak and let rest. Air fry onions for 10 mins.

7. Slice steak and serve with fried onions on top.

8. **Variations & Ingredients Tips**:

9. Use a different cut of steak like strip steak or tenderloin.

10. Add other herbs like rosemary or oregano to the marinade.

11. Toss the fried onions with a bit of balsamic glaze before serving.

12. **Per Serving**: 465 Calories; 27g Total Fat; 10g Saturated Fat; 108mg Cholesterol; 555mg Sodium; 17g Total Carbs; 2g Fiber; 10g Sugars; 37g Protein

Smokehouse-style Beef Ribs

Servings: 3
Prep Time: 5 Minutes | Cooking Time: 25 Minutes
Ingredients:

- 1 g Mild smoked paprika
- 1 g Garlic powder
- 1 g Onion powder
- 1 g Table salt
- 1 g Ground black pepper
- 3 283 g to 340 g beef back ribs (not beef short ribs)

Directions:

1. Preheat the air fryer to 175°C/350°F.

2. Mix the smoked paprika, garlic powder, onion powder, salt, and pepper in a small bowl until uniform. Massage and pat this mixture onto the ribs.

3. When the machine is at temperature, set the ribs in the basket in one layer, turning them on their sides if necessary, sort of like they're spooning but with at least 6 mm air space between them. Air-fry for 25 minutes, turning once, until deep brown and sizzling.

4. Use kitchen tongs to transfer the ribs to a wire rack. Cool for 5 minutes before serving.

5. **Variations & Ingredients Tips**:

6. Brush the ribs with your favorite BBQ sauce in the last 5 minutes of cooking

7. Sprinkle with chopped parsley or green onions before serving

8. Serve with coleslaw, potato salad and cornbread for a BBQ feast

9. **Per Serving**: Calories: 456; Total Fat: 35g; Saturated Fat: 14g; Cholesterol: 113mg; Sodium: 378mg; Total Carbs: 1g; Dietary Fiber: 0g; Total Sugars: 0g; Protein: 32g

Fish And Seafood Recipes

Shrimp Al Pesto

Servings: 4
Prep Time: 5 Minutes | Cooking Time: 10 Minutes
Ingredients:
- 450g peeled shrimp, deveined
- 1/4 cup pesto sauce
- 1 lime, sliced
- 2 cups cooked farro

Directions:
1. Preheat air fryer to 180°C/360°F.
2. Coat the shrimp with the pesto sauce in a bowl.
3. Put the shrimp in a single layer in the frying basket. Place the lime slices over the shrimp.
4. Roast for 5 minutes. Remove lime and discard.
5. Serve the shrimp over a bed of farro pilaf. Enjoy!
6. **Variations & Ingredients Tips**:
7. Use your favorite store-bought or homemade pesto.
8. Add cherry tomatoes or sliced zucchini to the basket.
9. Swap farro for rice, quinoa or pasta.
10. **Per serving**: Calories: 250; Total Fat: 9g; Saturated Fat: 2g; Cholesterol: 170mg; Sodium: 480mg; Total Carbs: 21g; Dietary Fiber: 3g; Sugars: 2g; Protein: 21g

Mediterranean Salmon Burgers

Servings: 4
Prep Time: 15 Minutes | Cooking Time: 30 Minutes
Ingredients:
- 450g salmon fillets
- 1 scallion, diced
- 4 tbsp mayonnaise
- 1 egg
- 1 tsp capers, drained
- Salt and pepper to taste
- 1/4 tsp paprika
- 1 lemon, zested
- 1 lemon, sliced
- 1 tbsp chopped dill
- 1/4 cup bread crumbs
- 4 buns, toasted
- 4 tsp whole-grain mustard
- 4 lettuce leaves
- 1 small tomato, sliced

Directions:
1. Preheat air fryer to 200°C/400°F.
2. Divide salmon in half. Cut one of the halves into chunks and transfer the chunks to the food processor. Also, add scallion, 2 tablespoons mayonnaise, egg, capers, dill, salt, pepper, paprika, and lemon zest. Pulse to puree.
3. Dice the rest of the salmon into 6mm chunks. Combine chunks and puree along with bread crumbs in a large bowl.
4. Shape the fish into 4 patties and transfer to the frying basket. Air Fry for 5 minutes, then flip the patties. Air Fry for another 5 to 7 minutes.
5. Place the patties each on a bun along with 1 teaspoon mustard, mayonnaise, lettuce, lemon slices, and a slice of tomato. Serve and enjoy.
6. **Variations & Ingredients Tips**:
7. Substitute Greek yogurt for some of the mayonnaise.
8. Add feta or olives to the salmon patty mixture.
9. Serve on pita bread instead of buns.
10. **Per serving**: Calories 450, Total Fat 23g, Saturated Fat 4g, Cholesterol 135mg, Sodium 620mg, Total Carbs 29g, Fiber 2g, Sugars 4g, Protein 34g

Caribbean Jerk Cod Fillets

Servings:2
Prep Time: 10 Minutes | Cooking Time: 20 Minutes
Ingredients:
- ¼ cup chopped cooked shrimp
- ¼ cup diced mango
- 1 tomato, diced
- 2 tbsp diced red onion
- 1 tbsp chopped parsley
- ¼ tsp ginger powder
- 2 tsp lime juice
- Salt and pepper to taste
- 2 cod fillets

- 2 tsp Jerk seasoning

Directions:
1. In a bowl, combine the shrimp, mango, tomato, red onion, parsley, ginger powder, lime juice, salt, and black pepper. Let chill the salsa in the fridge until ready to use.
2. Preheat air fryer to 180°C/350°F.
3. Sprinkle cod fillets with Jerk seasoning. Place them in the greased air fryer basket and Air Fry for 10 minutes or until the cod is opaque and flakes easily with a fork.
4. Divide between 2 medium plates. Serve topped with the Caribbean salsa.
5. **Variations & Ingredients Tips**:
6. Substitute cod with halibut, mahi-mahi, or snapper fillets.
7. Use pineapple or papaya instead of mango for a different tropical flavor.
8. Add a dash of hot sauce or minced jalapeño to the salsa for extra heat.
9. **Per Serving**: Calories: 200; Total Fat: 2g; Saturated Fat: 0g; Sodium: 530mg; Total Carbohydrates: 14g; Dietary Fiber: 2g; Total Sugars: 9g; Protein: 32g

Peanut-crusted Salmon

Servings: 4
Prep Time: 15 Minutes | Cooking Time: 30 Minutes
Ingredients:
- 4 salmon fillets
- 2 eggs, beaten
- 85g melted butter
- 1 garlic clove, minced
- 1 tsp lemon zest
- 1 lemon
- 1 tsp celery salt
- 1 tbsp parsley, chopped
- 1 tsp dill, chopped
- 1/2 cup peanuts, crushed

Directions:
1. Preheat air fryer to 175°C/350°F.
2. Put the beaten eggs, melted butter, lemon juice, lemon zest, garlic, parsley, celery salt, and dill in a bowl and stir thoroughly.
3. Dip in the salmon fillets, then roll them in the crushed peanuts, coating completely.

4. Place the coated salmon fillets in the frying basket.
5. Air Fry for 14-16 minutes, flipping once halfway through cooking, until the salmon is cooked through and the crust is toasted and crispy.
6. Serve.
7. **Variations & Ingredients Tips**:
8. Use other nuts like almonds or pecans instead of peanuts.
9. Add cayenne or chili powder to the coating for some heat.
10. Serve over a salad or with roasted vegetables.
11. **Per serving**: Calories: 550; Total Fat: 40g; Saturated Fat: 12g; Cholesterol: 180mg; Sodium: 450mg; Total Carbs: 14g; Dietary Fiber: 2g; Sugars: 2g; Protein: 35g

Lemon-dill Salmon Burgers

Servings: 4
Prep Time: 15 Minutes | Cooking Time: 8 Minutes
Ingredients:
- 2 (170g) fillets of salmon, finely chopped by hand or in a food processor
- 1 cup fine breadcrumbs
- 1 teaspoon freshly grated lemon zest
- 2 tablespoons chopped fresh dill weed
- 1 teaspoon salt
- Freshly ground black pepper
- 2 eggs, lightly beaten
- 4 brioche or hamburger buns
- Lettuce, tomato, red onion, avocado, mayonnaise or mustard, to serve

Directions:
1. Preheat the air fryer to 200°C/400°F.
2. Combine all the ingredients in a bowl. Mix together well and divide into four balls. Flatten the balls into patties, making an indentation in the center of each patty with your thumb (this will help the burger stay flat as it cooks) and flattening the sides of the burgers so that they fit nicely into the air fryer basket.
3. Transfer the burgers to the air fryer basket and air-fry for 4 minutes. Flip the burgers over and air-fry for another 3 to 4 minutes, until nicely browned and firm to the touch.
4. Serve on soft brioche buns with your choice of topping – lettuce, tomato, red onion, avocado, mayonnaise or mustard.
5. **Variations & Ingredients Tips**:

6. Use canned salmon or tuna instead of fresh for convenience.

7. Add some capers, olives or sun-dried tomatoes to the burger mix.

8. Top with a tangy tzatziki sauce or spicy remoulade.

9. **Per serving**: Calories: 430; Total Fat: 22g; Saturated Fat: 4.5g; Cholesterol: 170mg; Sodium: 890mg; Total Carbs: 32g; Dietary Fiber: 2g; Total Sugars: 5g; Protein: 28g

Cajun Flounder Fillets

Servings: 2
Prep Time: 5 Minutes | Cooking Time: 5 Minutes
Ingredients:

- 2 113-gram skinless flounder fillet(s)
- 2 teaspoons Peanut oil
- 1 teaspoon Purchased or homemade Cajun dried seasoning blend (see the headnote)

Directions:

1. Preheat the air fryer to 200°C/400°F.

2. Oil the fillet(s) by drizzling on the peanut oil, then gently rubbing in the oil with your clean, dry fingers. Sprinkle the seasoning blend evenly over both sides of the fillet(s).

3. When the machine is at temperature, set the fillet(s) in the basket. If working with more than one fillet, they should not touch, although they may be quite close together, depending on the basket's size. Air-fry undisturbed for 5 minutes, or until lightly browned and cooked through.

4. Use a nonstick-safe spatula to transfer the fillets to a serving platter or plate(s). Serve at once.

5. **Variations & Ingredients Tips**:

6. Substitute flounder with cod, tilapia, or catfish fillets.

7. Use olive oil or avocado oil instead of peanut oil for a different flavor.

8. Squeeze lemon or lime juice over the fillets after cooking for extra brightness.

9. **Per Serving**: Calories: 140; Total Fat: 7g; Saturated Fat: 1g; Sodium: 180mg; Total Carbohydrates: 0g; Dietary Fiber: 0g; Total Sugars: 0g; Protein: 19g

Fish Goujons With Tartar Sauce

Servings: 4
Prep Time: 10 Minutes | Cooking Time: 20 Minutes
Ingredients:

- 1/4 cup flour
- Salt and pepper to taste
- 1/4 tsp smoked paprika
- 1/4 tsp dried oregano
- 1 tsp dried thyme
- 1 egg
- 4 haddock fillets
- 1 lemon, thinly sliced
- 1/2 cup tartar sauce

Directions:

1. Preheat air fryer to 200°C/400°F.

2. Combine flour, salt, pepper, paprika, thyme, and oregano in a wide bowl. Whisk egg and 1 teaspoon water in another wide bowl.

3. Slice each fillet into 4 strips. Dip the strips in the egg mixture. Then roll them in the flour mixture and coat completely.

4. Arrange the fish strips on the greased frying basket. Air Fry for 4 minutes. Flip the fish and Air Fry for another 4 to 5 minutes until crisp.

5. Serve warm with lemon slices and tartar sauce on the side and enjoy.

6. **Variations & Ingredients Tips**:

7. Use cod, pollack or tilapia instead of haddock.

8. Season the flour with Old Bay, lemon pepper or Cajun spice.

9. Serve with malt vinegar, coleslaw or mushy peas.

10. **Per serving**: Calories: 330; Total Fat: 17g; Saturated Fat: 2.5g; Cholesterol: 140mg; Sodium: 570mg; Total Carbs: 14g; Dietary Fiber: 1g; Total Sugars: 1g; Protein: 30g

Beer-battered Cod

Servings: 3
Prep Time: 15 Minutes | Cooking Time: 12 Minutes
Ingredients:

- 1½ cups All-purpose flour
- 3 tablespoons Old Bay seasoning
- 1 large egg
- ¼ cup Amber beer, pale ale, or IPA
- 3 (115g) skinless cod fillets

- Vegetable oil spray

Directions:

1. Preheat the air fryer to 200°C/400°F.

2. Set up and fill two shallow soup plates or small pie plates on your counter: one with the flour, whisked with the Old Bay until well combined; and one with the egg, whisked with the beer until foamy and uniform.

3. Dip a piece of cod in the flour mixture, turning it to coat on all sides (not just the top and bottom). Gently shake off any excess flour and dip the fish in the egg mixture, turning it to coat. Let any excess egg mixture slip back into the rest, then set the fish back in the flour mixture and coat it again, then back in the egg mixture for a second wash, then back in the flour mixture for a third time. Coat the fish on all sides with vegetable oil spray and set it aside. "Batter" the remaining piece(s) of cod in the same way.

4. Set the coated cod fillets in the basket with as much space between them as possible. They should not touch. Air-fry undisturbed for 12 minutes, or until brown and crisp.

5. Use kitchen tongs to gently transfer the fish to a wire rack. Cool for only a couple of minutes before serving.

6. **Variations & Ingredients Tips**:

7. Use haddock, pollack or catfish instead of cod.

8. Substitute beer with sparkling water for a non-alcoholic version.

9. Serve with french fries, coleslaw and malt vinegar.

10. **Per serving**: Calories: 330; Total Fat: 5g; Saturated Fat: 1g; Cholesterol: 115mg; Sodium: 1120mg; Total Carbs: 44g; Dietary Fiber: 2g; Total Sugars: 1g; Protein: 26g

Home-style Fish Sticks

Servings: 4
Prep Time: 15 Minutes | Cooking Time: 30 Minutes
Ingredients:

- 450g cod fillets, cut into sticks
- 1 cup flour
- 1 egg
- 1/4 cup cornmeal
- Salt and pepper to taste
- 1/4 tsp smoked paprika
- 1 lemon

Directions:

1. Preheat air fryer at 175°C/350°F. In a bowl, add 1/2 cup of flour. In another bowl, beat the egg and in a third bowl, combine the remaining flour, cornmeal, salt, black pepper and paprika.

2. Roll the sticks in the flour, shake off excess flour. Then, dip them in the egg, shake off excess egg. Finally, dredge them in the cornmeal mixture.

3. Place fish fingers in the greased frying basket and Air Fry for 10 minutes, flipping once.

4. Serve with squeezed lemon.

5. **Variations & Ingredients Tips**:

6. Use haddock, pollock or tilapia instead of cod.

7. Substitute cornmeal with panko breadcrumbs for extra crunch.

8. Serve with tartar sauce, ketchup or ranch dressing for dipping.

9. **Per serving**: Calories: 260; Total Fat: 4g; Saturated Fat: 0.5g; Cholesterol: 100mg; Sodium: 200mg; Total Carbs: 29g; Dietary Fiber: 1g; Total Sugars: 0g; Protein: 28g

Asian-style Salmon Fillets

Servings: 4
Prep Time: 15 Minutes | Cooking Time: 15 Minutes
Ingredients:

- 1 tbsp sesame oil
- 2 tbsp miso paste
- 2 tbsp tamari
- 2 tbsp soy sauce
- 2 tbsp dark brown sugar
- 1/2 tsp garlic powder
- 1/2 tsp ginger powder
- 4 salmon fillets
- 4 cups cooked brown rice
- 4 lemon slices

Directions:

1. Preheat air fryer at 190°C/375°F. In a bowl, combine all ingredients, except for salmon and cooked rice.

2. Add 1/3 of the marinade to a shallow dish, submerge salmon fillets and let marinate covered in the fridge for 10 minutes. Reserve the remaining marinade.

3. Place salmon fillets, skin side up, in the greased frying basket and Air Fry for 6-8 minutes, turning once, and brush with the reserved marinade.

4. Divide cooked rice into serving dishes and top each with a salmon fillet. Pour the remaining marinade on top and serve with lemon slices on the side.

5. **Variations & Ingredients Tips**:

6. Use honey or maple syrup instead of brown sugar.

7. Add a sprinkle of toasted sesame seeds before serving.

8. Serve with stir-fried veggies or soba noodles.

9. **Per serving**: Calories: 510; Total Fat: 22g; Saturated Fat: 4g; Cholesterol: 95mg; Sodium: 1180mg; Total Carbs: 46g; Dietary Fiber: 3g; Total Sugars: 10g; Protein: 36g

Crab Stuffed Salmon Roast

Servings: 4
Prep Time: 15 Minutes | Cooking Time: 20 Minutes
Ingredients:

- 1 (680g) salmon fillet
- Salt and freshly ground black pepper
- 170g crabmeat
- 1 teaspoon finely chopped lemon zest
- 1 teaspoon Dijon mustard
- 1 tablespoon chopped fresh parsley, plus more for garnish
- 1 scallion, chopped
- 1/4 teaspoon salt
- Olive oil

Directions:

1. Prepare the salmon fillet by butterflying it. Slice into the thickest side of the salmon, parallel to the countertop and along the length of the fillet. Don't slice all the way through to the other side – stop about 2.5 cm from the edge. Open the salmon up like a book. Season the salmon with salt and freshly ground black pepper.

2. Make the crab filling by combining the crabmeat, lemon zest, mustard, parsley, scallion, salt and freshly ground black pepper in a bowl. Spread this filling in the center of the salmon. Fold one side of the salmon over the filling. Then fold the other side over on top.

3. Transfer the rolled salmon to the center of a piece of parchment paper that is roughly 15 cm wide and about 30 cm long. The parchment paper will act as a sling, making it easier to put the salmon into the air fryer. Preheat the air fryer to 190°C/370°F. Use the parchment paper to transfer the salmon roast to the air fryer basket and tuck the ends of the paper down beside the salmon. Drizzle a little olive oil on top and season with salt and pepper.

4. Air-fry the salmon at 190°C/370°F for 20 minutes.

5. Remove the roast from the air fryer and let it rest for a few minutes. Then, slice it, sprinkle some more lemon zest and parsley (or fresh chives) on top and serve.

6. **Variations & Ingredients Tips**:

7. Use a blend of crab and shrimp for the stuffing.

8. Add some finely diced red bell pepper to the filling for color.

9. Serve with lemon wedges and a side of roasted asparagus.

10. **Per serving**: Calories: 330; Total Fat: 19g; Saturated Fat: 3.5g; Cholesterol: 115mg; Sodium: 490mg; Total Carbs: 2g; Dietary Fiber: 0g; Total Sugars: 1g; Protein: 36g

Pecan-orange Crusted Striped Bass

Servings: 2
Prep Time: 15 Minutes | Cooking Time: 9 Minutes
Ingredients:

- Flour for dredging
- 2 egg whites, lightly beaten
- 1 cup pecans, chopped
- 1 teaspoon finely chopped orange zest, plus more for garnish
- 1/2 teaspoon salt
- 2 fillets striped bass
- Salt and freshly ground black pepper
- Vegetable or olive oil, in a spray bottle
- 1/2 cup fresh orange juice
- 1/4 cup heavy cream
- 1 sprig fresh thyme

Directions:

1. Set up 3 dishes: flour, egg whites, pecans mixed with orange zest and salt.

2. Season fish with salt and pepper. Coat in flour, egg white, then pecan mixture.

3. Preheat air fryer to 200°C/400°F.

4. Spray crusted fillets with oil and transfer to air fryer basket.

5. Air-fry 9 minutes, flipping halfway, until nuts are toasted and fish is firm.

6. For sauce: Simmer orange juice, cream and thyme for 5 minutes.

7. Serve fish over salad with orange zest and sauce if desired.

8. **Variations & Ingredients Tips**:

9. Use other firm white fish like halibut or cod.

10. Substitute almond or breadcrumb coating.

11. Add cayenne or chili powder to the coating.

12. **Per serving**: Calories: 540; Total Fat: 35g; Saturated Fat: 10g; Cholesterol: 120mg; Sodium: 450mg; Total Carbs: 24g; Dietary Fiber: 4g; Sugars: 9g; Protein: 36g

Spiced Shrimp Empanadas

Servings: 5
Prep Time: 15 Minutes | Cooking Time: 30 Minutes
Ingredients:

- 225g peeled and deveined shrimp, chopped
- 2 tbsp diced red bell peppers
- 1 shallot, minced
- 1 scallion, chopped
- 2 garlic cloves, minced
- 2 tbsp chopped cilantro
- 1/2 tbsp lemon juice
- 1/4 tsp sweet paprika
- 1/8 tsp salt
- 1/8 tsp red pepper flakes
- 1/4 tsp ground nutmeg
- 1 large egg, beaten
- 10 empanada discs

Directions:

1. Combine all ingredients except egg and discs in a bowl.

2. Beat egg with 1 tsp water in a small bowl.

3. Place 2 tbsp shrimp filling in center of each disc.

4. Brush edges with egg wash and fold in half to seal. Crimp with a fork.

5. Brush tops with egg wash.

6. Preheat air fryer to 190°C/380°F.

7. Place empanadas in greased basket. Air Fry 9 mins, flipping once, until golden.

8. Serve hot.

9. **Variations & Ingredients Tips**:

10. Use pie crust dough instead of empanada discs.

11. Add shredded cheese to the filling.

12. Serve with guacamole or sour cream for dipping.

13. **Per serving**: Calories: 180; Total Fat: 6g; Saturated Fat: 1g; Cholesterol: 95mg; Sodium: 280mg; Total Carbs: 22g; Dietary Fiber: 1g; Sugars: 1g; Protein: 10g

Garlic-lemon Steamer Clams

Servings: 2
Prep Time: 25 Minutes | Cooking Time: 30 Minutes
Ingredients:

- 25 Manila clams, scrubbed
- 2 tbsp butter, melted
- 1 garlic clove, minced
- 2 lemon wedges

Directions:

1. Add the clams to a large bowl filled with water and let sit for 10 minutes. Drain. Pour more water and let sit for 10 more minutes. Drain.

2. Preheat air fryer to 175°C/350°F. Place clams in the basket and Air Fry for 7 minutes. Discard any clams that don't open.

3. Remove clams from shells and place them into a large serving dish. Drizzle with melted butter and garlic and squeeze lemon on top.

4. Serve.

5. **Variations & Ingredients Tips**:

6. Add some white wine, shallots or parsley to the butter sauce.

7. Use littleneck or cherrystone clams instead of Manila.

8. Serve with crusty bread for dipping in the sauce.

9. **Per serving**: Calories: 270; Total Fat: 15g; Saturated Fat: 8g; Cholesterol: 75mg; Sodium: 180mg; Total Carbs: 9g; Dietary Fiber: 0g; Total Sugars: 0g; Protein: 25g

British Fish & Chips

Servings: 4
Prep Time: 20 Minutes | Cooking Time: 40 Minutes
Ingredients:

- 2 peeled russet potatoes, thinly sliced
- 1 egg white
- 1 tbsp lemon juice
- 1/3 cup ground almonds
- 2 bread slices, crumbled
- 1/2 tsp dried basil

- 4 haddock fillets

Directions:

1. Preheat air fryer to 200°C/390°F.
2. Lay the potato slices in the frying basket and Air Fry for 11-15 minutes. Turn the fries a couple of times while cooking.
3. While the fries are cooking, whisk the egg white and lemon juice together in a bowl. On a plate, combine the almonds, breadcrumbs, and basil.
4. First, one at a time, dip the fillets into the egg mix and then coat in the almond/breadcrumb mix. Lay the fillets on a wire rack until the fries are done.
5. Preheat the oven to 175°C/350°F. After the fries are done, move them to a pan and place in the oven to keep warm.
6. Put the fish in the frying basket and Air Fry for 10-14 minutes or until cooked through, golden, and crispy.
7. Serve with the fries.
8. **Variations & Ingredients Tips**:
9. Use cod, pollock or halibut instead of haddock.
10. Season the fish batter with salt, pepper and Old Bay seasoning.
11. Serve with malt vinegar, tartar sauce and mushy peas.
12. **Per serving**: Calories: 400; Total Fat: 17g; Saturated Fat: 2g; Cholesterol: 80mg; Sodium: 260mg; Total Carbs: 34g; Dietary Fiber: 5g; Total Sugars: 2g; Protein: 31g

Tuna Patties With Dill Sauce

Servings: 6
Prep Time: 40 Minutes | Cooking Time: 10 Minutes
Ingredients:

- Two (140g) cans albacore tuna, drained
- 1/2 teaspoon garlic powder
- 2 teaspoons dried dill, divided
- 1/2 teaspoon black pepper
- 1/2 teaspoon salt, divided
- 1/4 cup minced onion
- 1 large egg
- 7 tablespoons mayonnaise, divided
- 1/4 cup panko breadcrumbs
- 1 teaspoon fresh lemon juice
- 1/4 teaspoon fresh lemon zest
- 6 pieces butterleaf lettuce
- 1 cup diced tomatoes

Directions:

1. In a large bowl, mix the tuna with the garlic powder, 1 teaspoon of the dried dill, the black pepper, 1/4 teaspoon of the salt, and the onion. Make sure to use the back of a fork to really break up the tuna so there are no large chunks.
2. Mix in the egg and 1 tablespoon of the mayonnaise; then fold in the breadcrumbs so the tuna begins to form a thick batter that holds together.
3. Portion the tuna mixture into 6 equal patties and place on a plate lined with parchment paper in the refrigerator for at least 30 minutes. This will help the patties hold together in the air fryer.
4. When ready to cook, preheat the air fryer to 175°C/350°F.
5. Liberally spray the metal trivet that sits inside the air fryer basket with olive oil mist and place the patties onto the trivet.
6. Cook for 5 minutes, flip, and cook another 5 minutes.
7. While the patties are cooking, make the dill sauce by combining the remaining 6 tablespoons of mayonnaise with the remaining 1 teaspoon of dill, the lemon juice, the lemon zest, and the remaining 1/4 teaspoon of salt. Set aside.
8. Remove the patties from the air fryer.
9. Place 1 slice of lettuce on a plate and top with the tuna patty and a tomato slice. Repeat to form the remaining servings. Drizzle the dill dressing over the top. Serve immediately.
10. **Variations & Ingredients Tips**:
11. Add some diced celery or red bell pepper to the patty mix.
12. Use Greek yogurt instead of mayo for a lighter dill sauce.
13. Serve on toasted hamburger buns with sliced avocado.
14. **Per serving**: Calories: 200; Total Fat: 14g; Saturated Fat: 2.5g; Cholesterol: 60mg; Sodium: 480mg; Total Carbs: 6g; Dietary Fiber: 1g; Total Sugars: 2g; Protein: 12g

Buttery Lobster Tails

Servings: 4
Prep Time: 20 Minutes | Cooking Time: 6 Minutes
Ingredients:

- 4 170g to 225g shell-on raw lobster tails
- 2 tablespoons Butter, melted and cooled
- 1 teaspoon Lemon juice

- ½ teaspoon Finely grated lemon zest
- ½ teaspoon Garlic powder
- ½ teaspoon Table salt
- ½ teaspoon Ground black pepper

Directions:

1. Preheat the air fryer to 190°C/375°F.
2. To give the tails that restaurant look, you need to butterfly the meat. To do so, place a tail on a cutting board so that the shell is convex. Use kitchen shears to cut a line down the middle of the shell from the larger end to the smaller, cutting only the shell and not the meat below, and stopping before the back fins. Pry open the shell, leaving it intact. Use your clean fingers to separate the meat from the shell's sides and bottom, keeping it attached to the shell at the back near the fins. Pull the meat up and out of the shell through the cut line, laying the meat on top of the shell and closing the shell (as well as you can) under the meat. Make two equidistant cuts down the meat from the larger end to near the smaller end, each about 0.5cm deep, for the classic restaurant look on the plate. Repeat this procedure with the remaining tails.
3. Stir the butter, lemon juice, zest, garlic powder, salt, and pepper in a small bowl until well combined. Brush this mixture over the lobster meat set atop the shells.
4. When the machine is at temperature, place the tails shell side down in the basket with as much air space between them as possible. Air-fry undisturbed for 6 minutes, or until the lobster meat has pink streaks over it and is firm.
5. Use kitchen tongs to transfer the tails to a wire rack. Cool for only a minute or two before serving.
6. **Variations & Ingredients Tips**:
7. For extra kick, add a pinch of cayenne pepper or hot paprika to the butter mixture.
8. Substitute lime for lemon if you prefer a different citrus flavor.
9. Serve the lobster tails with melted garlic butter for dipping.
10. **Per serving**: Calories: 170; Total Fat: 8g; Saturated Fat: 4.5g; Cholesterol: 125mg; Sodium: 520mg; Total Carbohydrates: 1g; Dietary Fiber: 0g; Total Sugars: 0g; Protein: 23g

Beer-breaded Halibut Fish Tacos

Servings: 4

Prep Time: 40 Minutes | Cooking Time: 10 Minutes

Ingredients:

- 450g halibut, cut into 2.5-cm strips
- 1 cup light beer
- 1 jalapeño, minced and divided
- 1 clove garlic, minced
- 1/4 teaspoon ground cumin
- ½ cup cornmeal
- ¼ cup all-purpose flour
- 1¼ teaspoons sea salt, divided
- 2 cups shredded cabbage
- 1 lime, juiced and divided
- ¼ cup Greek yogurt
- ¼ cup Greek yogurt
- 1 cup grape tomatoes, quartered
- ½ cup chopped cilantro
- ¼ cup chopped onion
- 1 egg, whisked
- 8 corn tortillas

Directions:

1. In a shallow baking dish, place the fish, the beer, 1 teaspoon of the minced jalapeño, the garlic, and the cumin. Cover and refrigerate for 30 minutes.
2. Meanwhile, in a medium bowl, mix together the cornmeal, flour, and 1/2 teaspoon of the salt.
3. In large bowl, mix together the shredded cabbage, 1 tablespoon of the lime juice, the Greek yogurt, the mayonnaise, and 1/2 teaspoon of the salt.
4. In a small bowl, make the pico de gallo by mixing together the tomatoes, cilantro, onion, 1/4 teaspoon of the salt, the remaining jalapeño, and the remaining lime juice.
5. Remove the fish from the refrigerator and discard the marinade. Dredge the fish in the whisked egg; then dredge the fish in the cornmeal flour mixture, until all pieces of fish have been breaded.
6. Preheat the air fryer to 175°C/350°F.
7. Place the fish in the air fryer basket and spray liberally with cooking spray. Cook for 6 minutes, flip and shake the fish, and cook another 4 minutes.
8. While the fish is cooking, heat the tortillas in a heavy skillet for 1 to 2 minutes over high heat.
9. To assemble the tacos, place the battered fish on the heated tortillas, and top with slaw and pico de gallo. Serve immediately.
10. **Variations & Ingredients Tips**:
11. Use cod, tilapia or snapper instead of halibut.

12. Substitute the beer with sparkling water or ginger ale for a non-alcoholic version.

13. Add some sliced avocado or guacamole on top.

14. **Per serving**: Calories: 420; Total Fat: 18g; Saturated Fat: 4g; Cholesterol: 120mg; Sodium: 910mg; Total Carbs: 37g; Dietary Fiber: 5g; Total Sugars: 5g; Protein: 29g

Timeless Garlic-lemon Scallops

Servings: 2

Prep Time: 5 Minutes | Cooking Time: 15 Minutes

Ingredients:

- 2 tbsp butter, melted
- 1 garlic clove, minced
- 1 tbsp lemon juice
- 450g jumbo sea scallops

Directions:

1. Preheat air fryer to 200°C/400°F.

2. Whisk butter, garlic, and lemon juice in a bowl. Roll scallops in the mixture to coat all sides.

3. Place scallops in the frying basket and Air Fry for 4 minutes, flipping once. Brush the tops of each scallop with butter mixture and cook for 4 more minutes, flipping once.

4. Serve and enjoy!

5. **Variations & Ingredients Tips**:

6. Sprinkle scallops with Old Bay seasoning or smoked paprika.

7. Wrap each scallop with a slice of prosciutto before air frying.

8. Serve over angel hair pasta or creamy risotto.

9. **Per serving**: Calories: 290; Total Fat: 16g; Saturated Fat: 9g; Cholesterol: 100mg; Sodium: 990mg; Total Carbs: 5g; Dietary Fiber: 0g; Total Sugars: 0g; Protein: 33g

Pecan-crusted Tilapia

Servings: 4

Prep Time: 10 Minutes | Cooking Time: 8 Minutes

Ingredients:

- 450g skinless, boneless tilapia filets
- ¼ cup butter, melted
- 1 teaspoon minced fresh or dried rosemary
- 1 cup finely chopped pecans
- 1 teaspoon sea salt
- 1/4 teaspoon paprika
- 2 tablespoons chopped parsley
- 1 lemon, cut into wedges

Directions:

1. Pat the tilapia filets dry with paper towels.

2. Pour the melted butter over the filets and flip to coat them completely.

3. In a medium bowl, mix together the rosemary, pecans, salt, and paprika.

4. Preheat the air fryer to 175°C/350°F.

5. Place the tilapia filets into the air fryer basket and top with the pecan coating. Cook for 6 to 8 minutes until firm and flaky.

6. Remove the fish from the air fryer. Top with chopped parsley and serve with lemon wedges.

7. **Variations & Ingredients Tips**:

8. Use other nuts like almonds or walnuts instead of pecans.

9. Add parmesan or breadcrumbs to the nut coating.

10. Serve over a salad or with roasted vegetables.

11. **Per serving**: Calories: 330; Total Fat: 21g; Saturated Fat: 5g; Cholesterol: 85mg; Sodium: 520mg; Total Carbs: 9g; Dietary Fiber: 2g; Sugars: 1g; Protein: 27g

Vegetarian Recipes

Vegetarian Stuffed Bell Peppers

Servings: 3
Prep Time: 15 Minutes | Cooking Time: 40 Minutes
Ingredients:
- 1 cup mushrooms, chopped
- 1 tbsp allspice
- 3/4 cup Alfredo sauce
- 1/2 cup canned diced tomatoes
- 1 cup cooked rice
- 2 tbsp dried parsley
- 2 tbsp hot sauce
- Salt and pepper to taste
- 3 large bell peppers

Directions:
1. Preheat air fryer to 190°C/375°F.
2. Whisk mushrooms, allspice and 1 cup of boiling water until smooth.
3. Stir in Alfredo sauce, tomatoes and juices, rice, parsley, hot sauce, salt, and black pepper. Set aside.
4. Cut the top of each bell pepper, take out the core and seeds without breaking the pepper.
5. Fill each pepper with the rice mixture and cover them with a 15-cm square of aluminum foil, folding the edges.
6. Roast for 30 minutes until tender.
7. Let cool completely before unwrapping. Serve immediately.
8. **Variations & Ingredients Tips:**
9. Use different grains like quinoa or farro instead of rice.
10. Add vegan cheese shreds to the filling.
11. Top with vegan sour cream or cashew cream.
12. **Per Serving:** Calories: 316; Total Fat: 14g; Saturated Fat: 3g; Sodium: 1156mg; Total Carbohydrates: 42g; Dietary Fiber: 5g; Total Sugars: 10g; Protein: 8g

Fried Rice With Curried Tofu

Servings: 4
Prep Time: 10 Minutes | Cooking Time: 25 Minutes
Ingredients:

- 225g extra-firm tofu, cubed
- 1/2 cup canned coconut milk
- 2 tsp red curry paste
- 2 cloves garlic, minced
- 1 tbsp avocado oil
- 1 tbsp coconut oil
- 2 cups cooked rice
- 1 tbsp turmeric powder
- Salt and pepper to taste
- 4 lime wedges
- 1/4 cup chopped cilantro

Directions:
1. Preheat air fryer to 175°C/350°F.
2. Combine tofu, coconut milk, curry paste, garlic, and avocado oil in a bowl. Pour the mixture into a baking pan. Place the pan in the frying basket and Air Fry for 10 minutes, stirring once.
3. Melt the coconut oil in a skillet over medium heat. Add in rice, turmeric powder, salt, and black pepper, and cook for 2 minutes or until heated through.
4. Divide the cooked rice between 4 medium bowls and top with tofu mixture and sauce. Top with cilantro and lime wedges to serve.
5. **Variations & Ingredients Tips:**
6. Use brown rice or quinoa for extra fiber and nutrients.
7. Add diced bell peppers or carrots for extra veggies.
8. Top with cashews or peanuts for a crunchy texture.
9. **Per Serving:** Calories: 330; Total Fat: 21g; Saturated Fat: 9g; Sodium: 125mg; Total Carbs: 27g; Dietary Fiber: 3g; Total Sugars: 1g; Protein: 11g

Broccoli Cheddar Stuffed Potatoes

Servings: 2
Prep Time: 15 Minutes | Cooking Time: 42 Minutes
Ingredients:
- 2 large russet potatoes, scrubbed
- 1 tablespoon olive oil
- salt and freshly ground black pepper
- 2 tablespoons butter
- ¼ cup sour cream

- 3 tablespoons half-and-half (or milk)
- 1¼ cups grated Cheddar cheese, divided
- ¾ teaspoon salt
- freshly ground black pepper
- 1 cup frozen baby broccoli florets, thawed and drained

Directions:

1. Preheat the air fryer to 200℃/400°F.

2. Rub the potatoes all over with olive oil and season generously with salt and freshly ground black pepper. Transfer the potatoes into the air fryer basket and air-fry for 30 minutes, turning the potatoes over halfway through the cooking process.

3. Remove the potatoes from the air fryer and let them rest for 5 minutes. Cut a large oval out of the top of both potatoes. Leaving 1.25 cm of potato flesh around the edge of the potato, scoop the inside of the potato out and into a large bowl to prepare the potato filling. Mash the scooped potato filling with a fork and add the butter, sour cream, half-and-half, 120 grams of the grated Cheddar cheese, salt and pepper to taste. Mix well and then fold in the broccoli florets.

4. Stuff the hollowed out potato shells with the potato and broccoli mixture. Mound the filling high in the potatoes – you will have more filling than room in the potato shells.

5. Transfer the stuffed potatoes back to the air fryer basket and air-fry at 180℃/360°F for 10 minutes. Sprinkle the remaining Cheddar cheese on top of each stuffed potato, lower the heat to 165℃/330°F and air-fry for an additional minute or two to melt cheese.

6. **Variations & Ingredients Tips**:

7. Add chopped bacon, ham, or prosciutto to the potato filling for a meaty flavor.

8. Substitute broccoli with cauliflower, spinach, or kale for different veggie options.

9. Top with chopped chives, scallions, or parsley for a fresh garnish.

10. **Per Serving** (1 stuffed potato): Calories: 630; Cholesterol: 85mg; Total Fat: 41g; Saturated Fat: 22g; Sodium: 1470mg; Total Carbohydrates: 49g; Dietary Fiber: 5g; Total Sugars: 3g; Protein: 22g

Mushroom-rice Stuffed Bell Peppers

Servings: 4
Prep Time: 20 Minutes | Cooking Time: 30 Minutes

Ingredients:

- 4 red bell peppers, tops sliced
- 1 ½ cups cooked rice
- ¼ cup chopped leeks
- ¼ cup sliced mushrooms
- ¾ cup tomato sauce
- Salt and pepper to taste
- ¾ cup shredded mozzarella
- 2 tbsp parsley, chopped

Directions:

1. Fill a large pot of water and heat on high until it boils. Remove seeds and membranes from the peppers. Carefully place peppers into the boiling water for 5 minutes. Remove and set aside to cool.

2. Mix together rice, leeks, mushrooms, tomato sauce, parsley, salt, and pepper in a large bowl. Stuff each pepper with the rice mixture. Top with mozzarella.

3. Preheat air fryer to 180°C/350°F. Arrange the peppers on the greased air fryer basket and Bake for 10 minutes. Serve.

4. **Variations & Ingredients Tips**:

5. Use quinoa, couscous, or cauliflower rice instead of regular rice.

6. Add ground veggie crumbles or lentils for more protein.

7. Top with hot sauce or sriracha for a spicy touch.

8. **Per Serving**: Calories: 210; Total Fat: 6g; Saturated Fat: 3.5g; Sodium: 420mg; Total Carbohydrates: 29g; Dietary Fiber: 4g; Total Sugars: 8g; Protein: 11g

Effortless Mac `n´ Cheese

Servings: 4
Prep Time: 10 Minutes | Cooking Time: 15 Minutes

Ingredients:

- 1 cup heavy cream
- 1 cup milk
- ½ cup mozzarella cheese
- 2 tsp grated Parmesan cheese
- 455 grams cooked elbow macaroni

Directions:

1. Preheat air fryer to 200℃/400°F. Whisk the heavy cream, milk, mozzarella cheese, and Parmesan cheese until smooth in a bowl. Stir in the macaroni and pour into a baking dish. Cover with foil and Bake in the air

fryer for 6 minutes. Remove foil and Bake until cooked through and bubbly, 3-5 minutes. Serve warm.

2. **Variations & Ingredients Tips**:

3. Add diced jalapeños, bacon bits, or breadcrumbs for extra flavor and texture.

4. Substitute elbow macaroni with penne, fusilli, or shells for a different pasta shape.

5. Use a combination of different cheeses like cheddar, gouda, or Gruyère for a more complex flavor.

6. **Per Serving**: Calories: 640; Cholesterol: 125mg; Total Fat: 41g; Saturated Fat: 25g; Sodium: 360mg; Total Carbohydrates: 46g; Dietary Fiber: 2g; Total Sugars: 7g; Protein: 22g

Curried Cauliflower

Servings: 2
Prep Time: 10 Minutes | Cooking Time: 30 Minutes
Ingredients:

- 1 cup canned diced tomatoes
- 2 cups milk
- 2 tbsp lime juice
- 1 tbsp allspice
- 1 tbsp curry powder
- 1 tsp ground ginger
- 1/2 tsp ground cumin
- 340 grams frozen cauliflower
- 455 grams cheddar cheese, cubed
- 1/4 cup chopped cilantro

Directions:

1. Preheat air fryer to 190°C/375°F.

2. Combine the tomatoes and their juices, milk, lime juice, allspice, curry powder, ginger, and cumin in a baking pan.

3. Toss in cauliflower and cheddar cheese until coated.

4. Roast for 15 minutes, stir and Roast for another 10 minutes until bubbly.

5. Scatter with cilantro before serving.

6. **Variations & Ingredients Tips**:

7. Add diced potatoes, chickpeas, or tofu for extra texture and protein.

8. Substitute cheddar with paneer or a vegan cheese alternative.

9. Serve over basmati rice or with naan bread for a complete meal.

10. **Per Serving**: Calories: 780; Cholesterol: 180mg; Total Fat: 54g; Saturated Fat: 33g; Sodium: 1480mg;

Total Carbohydrates: 34g; Dietary Fiber: 7g; Total Sugars: 20g; Protein: 46g

Roasted Vegetable Thai Green Curry

Servings: 4
Prep Time: 15 Minutes | Cooking Time: 16 Minutes
Ingredients:

- 1 (400-ml) can coconut milk
- 3 tablespoons green curry paste
- 1 tablespoon soy sauce*
- 1 tablespoon rice wine vinegar
- 1 teaspoon sugar
- 1 teaspoon minced fresh ginger
- ½ onion, chopped
- 3 carrots, sliced
- 1 red bell pepper, chopped
- olive oil
- 10 stalks of asparagus, cut into 5-cm pieces
- 3 cups broccoli florets
- basmati rice for serving
- fresh cilantro
- crushed red pepper flakes (optional)

Directions:

1. Combine the coconut milk, green curry paste, soy sauce, rice wine vinegar, sugar and ginger in a medium saucepan and bring to a boil on the stovetop. Reduce the heat and simmer for 20 minutes while you cook the vegetables. Set aside.

2. Preheat the air fryer to 200°C/400°F.

3. Toss the onion, carrots, and red pepper together with a little olive oil and transfer the vegetables to the air fryer basket. Air-fry at 200°C/400°F for 10 minutes, shaking the basket a few times during the cooking process.

4. Add the asparagus and broccoli florets and air-fry for an additional 6 minutes, again shaking the basket for even cooking.

5. When the vegetables are cooked to your liking, toss them with the green curry sauce and serve in bowls over basmati rice. Garnish with fresh chopped cilantro and crushed red pepper flakes.

6. **Variations & Ingredients Tips**:

7. Use yellow or red curry paste for a different flavor profile.

8. Add cubed tofu or tempeh for extra protein.

9. Serve with quinoa or rice noodles instead of basmati rice.

10. **Per Serving**: Calories: 420; Total Fat: 32g; Saturated Fat: 25g; Sodium: 680mg; Total Carbohydrates: 30g; Dietary Fiber: 7g; Total Sugars: 8g; Protein: 8g

Pinto Bean Casserole

Servings: 2

Prep Time: 5 Minutes | Cooking Time: 15 Minutes

Ingredients:
- 1 can pinto beans
- ¼ cup tomato sauce
- 2 tbsp cornstarch
- 2 garlic cloves, minced
- ½ tsp dried oregano
- ½ tsp cumin
- 1 tsp smoked paprika
- Salt and pepper to taste

Directions:
1. Preheat air fryer to 200°C/390°F.
2. Stir the beans, tomato sauce, cornstarch, garlic, oregano, cumin, smoked paprika, salt, and pepper in a bowl until combined.
3. Pour the bean mix into a greased baking pan.
4. Bake in the fryer for 4 minutes. Remove, stir, and Bake for 4 minutes or until the mix is thick and heated through.
5. Serve hot.
6. **Variations & Ingredients Tips**:
7. Top with shredded cheese, sour cream, and chopped cilantro.
8. Add diced bell peppers and onions for extra veggies.
9. Use black beans or kidney beans for variation.
10. **Per Serving**: Calories: 280; Total Fat: 1.5g; Saturated Fat: 0g; Sodium: 980mg; Total Carbohydrates: 52g; Dietary Fiber: 15g; Total Sugars: 2g; Protein: 15g

Charred Cauliflower Tacos

Servings: 4

Prep Time: 15 Minutes | Cooking Time: 10 Minutes

Ingredients:
- 1 head cauliflower, washed and cut into florets
- 2 tablespoons avocado oil
- 2 teaspoons taco seasoning
- 1 medium avocado
- ½ teaspoon garlic powder
- ¼ teaspoon black pepper
- ¼ teaspoon salt
- 2 tablespoons chopped red onion
- 2 teaspoons fresh squeezed lime juice
- ¼ cup chopped cilantro
- Eight 15-cm corn tortillas
- ½ cup cooked corn
- ½ cup shredded purple cabbage

Directions:
1. Preheat the air fryer to 200℃/390°F.
2. In a large bowl, toss the cauliflower with the avocado oil and taco seasoning. Set the metal trivet inside the air fryer basket and liberally spray with olive oil.
3. Place the cauliflower onto the trivet and cook for 10 minutes, shaking every 3 minutes to allow for an even char.
4. While the cauliflower is cooking, prepare the avocado sauce. In a medium bowl, mash the avocado; then mix in the garlic powder, pepper, salt, and onion. Stir in the lime juice and cilantro; set aside.
5. Remove the cauliflower from the air fryer basket.
6. Place 1 tablespoon of avocado sauce in the middle of a tortilla, and top with corn, cabbage, and charred cauliflower. Repeat with the remaining tortillas. Serve immediately.
7. **Variations & Ingredients Tips**:
8. Use broccoli, Brussels sprouts, or carrots instead of cauliflower for different veggie options.
9. Add sliced radish, pickled onions, or queso fresco for extra toppings.
10. Serve with salsa, hot sauce, or lime wedges on the side.
11. **Per Serving** (2 tacos): Calories: 380; Cholesterol: 0mg; Total Fat: 20g; Saturated Fat: 3g; Sodium: 520mg; Total Carbohydrates: 47g; Dietary Fiber: 11g; Total Sugars: 7g; Protein: 8g

Roasted Vegetable, Brown Rice And Black Bean Burrito

Servings: 2

Prep Time: 10 Minutes | Cooking Time: 20 Minutes

Ingredients:

- 1/2 zucchini, sliced 0.6 cm thick
- 1/2 red onion, sliced
- 1 yellow bell pepper, sliced
- 2 teaspoons olive oil
- Salt and freshly ground black pepper
- 2 burrito size flour tortillas
- 1 cup grated pepper jack cheese
- 1/2 cup cooked brown rice
- 1/2 cup canned black beans, drained and rinsed
- 1/4 teaspoon ground cumin
- 1 tablespoon chopped fresh cilantro
- Fresh salsa, guacamole and sour cream, for serving

Directions:

1. Preheat air fryer to 200°C/400°F.
2. Toss veggies with oil, salt and pepper. Air fry 12-15 mins, shaking occasionally until tender.
3. Lay out tortillas and sprinkle half the cheese in the center.
4. Mix rice, beans, cumin, cilantro and season. Divide between tortillas.
5. Top with roasted veggies and remaining cheese. Roll up burritos.
6. Brush or spray outsides with oil. Air fry at 180°C/360°F for 8 mins, flipping halfway.
7. Serve warm with salsa, guacamole and sour cream.
8. **Variations & Ingredients Tips**:
9. Use whole wheat or spinach tortillas.
10. Substitute black beans with pinto or kidney beans.
11. Add sautéed mushrooms or diced avocado to filling.
12. **Per Serving**: Calories: 631; Total Fat: 28g; Saturated Fat: 13g; Sodium: 934mg; Total Carbohydrates: 72g; Dietary Fiber: 13g; Total Sugars: 6g; Protein: 25g

Spinach & Brie Frittata

Servings:4
Prep Time: 10 Minutes | Cooking Time: 25 Minutes
Ingredients:

- 5 eggs
- Salt and pepper to taste
- ½ cup baby spinach
- 1 shallot, diced
- 113 grams brie cheese, cubed
- 1 tomato, sliced

Directions:

1. Preheat air fryer to 160°C/320°F.
2. Whisk all ingredients, except for the tomato slices, in a bowl.
3. Transfer to a baking pan greased with olive oil and top with tomato slices.
4. Place the pan in the air fryer basket and Bake for 14 minutes.
5. Let cool for 5 minutes before slicing. Serve and enjoy!
6. **Variations & Ingredients Tips**:
7. Substitute brie with goat cheese, feta, or cheddar.
8. Add sliced mushrooms, bell peppers, or zucchini to the mix.
9. Top with sliced avocado or a dollop of sour cream.
10. **Per Serving**: Calories: 220; Total Fat: 16g; Saturated Fat: 8g; Sodium: 320mg; Total Carbohydrates: 3g; Dietary Fiber: 0g; Total Sugars: 2g; Protein: 15g

Healthy Living Mushroom Enchiladas

Servings: 4
Prep Time: 20 Minutes | Cooking Time: 40 Minutes
Ingredients:

- 2 cups sliced mushrooms
- ½ onion, thinly sliced
- 2 garlic cloves, minced
- 1 tbsp olive oil
- 280 grams spinach, chopped
- ½ tsp ground cumin
- 1 tbsp dried oregano
- 1 tsp chili powder
- ¼ cup grated feta cheese
- ¼ tsp red pepper flakes
- 1 cup grated mozzarella cheese
- 1 cup sour cream
- 2 tbsp mayonnaise
- Juice of 1 lime
- Salt and pepper to taste
- 8 corn tortillas
- 1 jalapeño pepper, diced
- ¼ cup chopped cilantro

Directions:

1. Preheat air fryer to 200°C/400°F.
2. Combine mushrooms, onion, oregano, garlic, chili powder, olive oil, and salt in a small bowl until well

coated. Transfer to the greased air fryer basket. Cook for 5 minutes, then shake the basket. Cook for another 3 to 4 minutes, then transfer to a medium bowl.

3. Wipe out the air fryer basket. Take the garlic cloves from the mushroom mixture and finely mince them. Return half of the garlic to the bowl with the mushrooms. Stir in spinach, cumin, red pepper flakes, and ½ cup of mozzarella.

4. Place the other half of the minced garlic in a small bowl along with sour cream, mayonnaise, feta, the rest of the mozzarella, lime juice, and black pepper.

5. To prepare the enchiladas, spoon 2 tablespoons of mushroom mixture in the center of each tortilla. Roll the tortilla and place it seam-side down in the baking dish. Repeat for the rest of the tortillas.

6. Top with sour cream mixture and garnish with jalapeños. Place the dish in the air fryer basket and bake for 20 minutes until heated through and just brown on top.

7. Top with cilantro. Serve.

8. **Variations & Ingredients Tips**:

9. Substitute mushrooms with zucchini, eggplant, or bell peppers for different veggie options.

10. Use flour tortillas instead of corn tortillas for a softer texture.

11. Add black beans, corn, or rice to the filling for extra heartiness.

12. **Per Serving**: Calories: 450; Cholesterol: 55mg; Total Fat: 31g; Saturated Fat: 13g; Sodium: 620mg; Total Carbohydrates: 34g; Dietary Fiber: 6g; Total Sugars: 7g; Protein: 16g

Veggie-stuffed Bell Peppers

Servings: 4
Prep Time: 15 Minutes | Cooking Time: 40 Minutes
Ingredients:

- 1/2 cup canned fire-roasted diced tomatoes, including juice
- 2 red bell peppers
- 4 tsp olive oil
- 1/2 yellow onion, diced
- 1 zucchini, diced
- 3/4 cup chopped mushrooms
- 1/4 cup tomato sauce
- 2 tsp Italian seasoning
- 1/4 tsp smoked paprika
- Salt and pepper to taste

Directions:

1. Cut bell peppers in half from top to bottom and discard the seeds. Brush inside and tops of the bell peppers with some olive oil. Set aside.

2. Warm the remaining olive oil in a skillet over medium heat. Stir-fry the onion, zucchini, and mushrooms for 5 minutes until the onions are tender.

3. Combine tomatoes and their juice, tomato sauce, Italian seasoning, paprika, salt, and pepper in a bowl.

4. Preheat air fryer to 180°C/350°F.

5. Divide both mixtures between bell pepper halves.

6. Place bell pepper halves in the frying basket and Air Fry for 8 minutes.

7. Serve immediately.

8. **Variations & Ingredients Tips**:

9. Add cooked grains like quinoa or rice for extra protein and fiber.

10. Use different cheese like vegan feta or cheddar shreds.

11. Substitute bell peppers with portobello mushroom caps.

12. **Per Serving**: Calories: 113; Total Fat: 6g; Saturated Fat: 1g; Sodium: 179mg; Total Carbohydrates: 13g; Dietary Fiber: 4g; Total Sugars: 7g; Protein: 3g

Falafel

Servings: 4
Prep Time: 15 Minutes | Cooking Time: 10 Minutes
Ingredients:

- One 400-gram can garbanzo beans (chickpeas), drained and rinsed
- 1 clove garlic, chopped
- 1 cup chopped parsley
- ½ cup chopped dill
- ½ teaspoon ground cumin
- ½ teaspoon ground coriander
- 1 teaspoon salt
- ¼ cup sesame seeds
- ½ cup breadcrumbs

Directions:

1. Preheat the air fryer to 175℃/350°F.

2. Pat the garbanzo beans dry with a towel. In a food processor, place the beans, garlic, parsley, dill, cumin, coriander, and salt. Blend for 2 minutes, scraping down the sides of the food processor every 30 seconds.

3. In a small bowl, mix together the breadcrumbs and sesame seeds. Working one at a time and using a cookie scoop or approximately 2 tablespoons, form a patty about 1.25-cm thick and round. Dredge the patties in the breadcrumb mixture.

4. Place the falafel in the air fryer basket, making sure they don't overlap. Spray with cooking spray and cook for 6 minutes, flip over, and cook another 4 to 6 minutes. Cook in batches as needed.

5. **Variations & Ingredients Tips**:

6. Add diced onions, red pepper flakes, or lemon juice to the falafel mixture for extra flavor.

7. Serve in a pita with lettuce, tomato, and tzatziki sauce for a classic falafel sandwich.

8. Use a mixture of chickpeas and fava beans for a more authentic taste.

9. **Per Serving** (3 falafel): Calories: 250; Cholesterol: 0mg; Total Fat: 8g; Saturated Fat: 1g; Sodium: 770mg; Total Carbohydrates: 36g; Dietary Fiber: 8g; Total Sugars: 5g; Protein: 11g

Tomato & Squash Stuffed Mushrooms

Servings:2
Prep Time: 10 Minutes | Cooking Time: 15 Minutes
Ingredients:

- 12 whole white button mushrooms
- 3 tsp olive oil
- 2 tbsp diced zucchini
- 1 tsp soy sauce
- ¼ tsp salt
- 2 tbsp tomato paste
- 1 tbsp chopped parsley

Directions:

1. Preheat air fryer to 180°C/350°F.

2. Remove the stems from the mushrooms. Chop the stems finely and set in a bowl. Brush 1 tsp of olive oil around the top ridge of mushroom caps.

3. To the bowl of the stem, add all ingredients, except for parsley, and mix.

4. Divide and press mixture into tops of mushroom caps.

5. Place the mushrooms in the air fryer basket and Air Fry for 5 minutes.

6. Top with parsley. Serve.

7. **Variations & Ingredients Tips**:

8. Use portobello mushrooms instead of button mushrooms for a larger appetizer.

9. Substitute zucchini with eggplant, yellow squash, or bell peppers.

10. Add grated Parmesan cheese or bread crumbs to the filling for extra flavor and texture.

11. **Per Serving**: Calories: 130; Total Fat: 10g; Saturated Fat: 1.5g; Sodium: 490mg; Total Carbohydrates: 7g; Dietary Fiber: 2g; Total Sugars: 4g; Protein: 4g

Tex-mex Potatoes With Avocado Dressing

Servings: 2
Prep Time: 20 Minutes | Cooking Time: 60 Minutes
Ingredients:

- ¼ cup chopped parsley, dill, cilantro, chives
- ¼ cup yogurt
- ½ avocado, diced
- 2 tbsp milk
- 2 tsp lemon juice
- ½ tsp lemon zest
- 1 green onion, chopped
- 2 cloves garlic, quartered
- Salt and pepper to taste
- 2 tsp olive oil
- 2 russet potatoes, scrubbed and perforated with a fork
- 1 cup steamed broccoli florets
- ½ cup canned white beans

Directions:

1. In a food processor, blend the yogurt, avocado, milk, lemon juice, lemon zest, green onion, garlic, parsley, dill, cilantro, chives, salt and pepper until smooth. Transfer it to a small bowl and let chill the dressing covered in the fridge until ready to use.

2. Preheat air fryer at 200°C/400°F. Rub olive oil over both potatoes and sprinkle with salt and pepper. Place them in the air fryer basket and Bake for 45 minutes, flipping at 30 minutes mark.

3. Let cool onto a cutting board for 5 minutes until cool enough to handle. Cut each potato lengthwise into slices and pinch ends together to open up each slice.

4. Stuff broccoli and beans into potatoes and put them back into the basket, and cook for 3 more minutes.

5. Drizzle avocado dressing over and serve.
6. **Variations & Ingredients Tips**:
7. Substitute russet potatoes with sweet potatoes or yams.
8. Use cauliflower florets or asparagus instead of broccoli.
9. Add cooked quinoa or brown rice to the stuffing.
10. **Per Serving**: Calories: 450; Total Fat: 18g; Saturated Fat: 3g; Sodium: 250mg; Total Carbohydrates: 64g; Dietary Fiber: 12g; Total Sugars: 5g; Protein: 14g

Balsamic Caprese Hasselback

Servings: 4
Prep Time: 10 Minutes | Cooking Time: 15 Minutes
Ingredients:

- 4 tomatoes
- 12 fresh basil leaves
- 1 ball fresh mozzarella
- Salt and pepper to taste
- 1 tbsp olive oil
- 2 tsp balsamic vinegar
- 1 tbsp basil, torn

Directions:
1. Preheat air fryer to 165℃/325°F. Remove the bottoms from the tomatoes to create a flat surface. Make 4 even slices on each tomato, 3/4 of the way down. Slice the mozzarella and then cut into 12 pieces. Stuff 1 basil leaf and a piece of mozzarella into each slice. Sprinkle with salt and pepper. Place the stuffed tomatoes in the frying basket and Air Fry for 3 minutes. Transfer to a large serving plate. Drizzle with olive oil and balsamic vinegar and scatter the basil over. Serve and enjoy!
2. **Variations & Ingredients Tips**:
3. Use cherry or grape tomatoes for bite-sized appetizers.
4. Substitute mozzarella with provolone or fontina cheese for a different flavor.
5. Add a drizzle of pesto or balsamic glaze for extra richness.
6. **Per Serving**: Calories: 160; Cholesterol: 25mg; Total Fat: 11g; Saturated Fat: 5g; Sodium: 220mg; Total Carbohydrates: 8g; Dietary Fiber: 2g; Total Sugars: 5g; Protein: 8g

Spinach And Cheese Calzone

Servings: 2
Prep Time: 20 Minutes | Cooking Time: 10 Minutes
Ingredients:

- ⅔ cup frozen chopped spinach, thawed
- 1 cup grated mozzarella cheese
- 1 cup ricotta cheese
- ½ teaspoon Italian seasoning
- ½ teaspoon salt
- freshly ground black pepper
- 1 store-bought or homemade pizza dough* (about 340 to 454 grams)
- 2 tablespoons olive oil
- pizza or marinara sauce (optional)

Directions:
1. Drain and squeeze all the water out of the thawed spinach and set it aside. Mix the mozzarella cheese, ricotta cheese, Italian seasoning, salt and freshly ground black pepper together in a bowl. Stir in the chopped spinach.
2. Divide the dough in half. With floured hands or on a floured surface, stretch or roll one half of the dough into a 25-cm circle. Spread half of the cheese and spinach mixture on half of the dough, leaving about 5 cm of dough empty around the edge.
3. Fold the other half of the dough over the cheese mixture, almost to the edge of the bottom dough to form a half moon. Fold the bottom edge of dough up over the top edge and crimp the dough around the edges in order to make the crust and seal the calzone. Brush the dough with olive oil. Repeat with the second half of dough to make the second calzone.
4. Preheat the air fryer to 180°C/360°F.
5. Brush or spray the air fryer basket with olive oil. Air-fry the calzones one at a time for 10 minutes, flipping the calzone over half way through. Serve with warm pizza or marinara sauce if desired.
6. **Variations & Ingredients Tips**:
7. Add sautéed mushrooms, onions, or bell peppers to the filling.
8. Use a combination of different cheeses like feta, provolone, or Parmesan.
9. Brush the calzone with garlic butter or sprinkle with Italian seasoning before air frying.
10. **Per Serving**: Calories: 790; Total Fat: 41g; Saturated Fat: 19g; Sodium: 1480mg; Total Carbohydrates: 70g; Dietary Fiber: 4g; Total Sugars: 4g; Protein: 38g

Pizza Margherita With Spinach

Servings: 4
Prep Time: 30 Minutes | Cooking Time: 50 Minutes

Ingredients:

- ½ cup pizza sauce
- 1 tsp dried oregano
- 1 tsp garlic powder
- 1 pizza dough
- 1 cup baby spinach
- ½ cup mozzarella cheese

Directions:

1. Preheat air fryer to 200°C/400°F.
2. Whisk pizza sauce, oregano, and garlic in a bowl. Set aside.
3. Form 4 balls with the pizza dough and roll out each into a 15-cm round pizza.
4. Lay one crust in the basket, spread ¼ of the sauce, then scatter with ¼ of spinach, and finally top with mozzarella cheese.
5. Grill for 8 minutes until golden brown and the crust is crispy.
6. Repeat the process with the remaining crusts. Serve immediately.
7. **Variations & Ingredients Tips**:
8. Add sliced cherry tomatoes, mushrooms, or bell peppers as additional toppings.
9. Sprinkle with red pepper flakes for some heat.
10. Brush the crust with garlic butter before adding toppings for extra flavor.
11. **Per Serving**: Calories: 280; Total Fat: 9g; Saturated Fat: 3.5g; Sodium: 520mg; Total Carbohydrates: 39g; Dietary Fiber: 2g; Total Sugars: 4g; Protein: 11g

Tofu & Spinach Lasagna

Servings: 4
Prep Time: 20 Minutes | Cooking Time: 30 Minutes

Ingredients:

- 227 grams cooked lasagne noodles
- 1 tbsp olive oil
- 2 cups crumbled tofu
- 2 cups fresh spinach
- 2 tbsp cornstarch
- 1 tsp onion powder
- Salt and pepper to taste
- 2 garlic cloves, minced
- 2 cups marinara sauce
- ½ cup shredded mozzarella

Directions:

1. Warm the olive oil in a large pan over medium heat. Add the tofu and spinach and stir-fry for a minute. Add the cornstarch, onion powder, salt, pepper, and garlic. Stir until the spinach wilts. Remove from heat.
2. Preheat air fryer to 200°C/390°F.
3. Pour a thin layer of pasta sauce in a baking pan. Layer 2-3 lasagne noodles on top of the marinara sauce. Top with a little more sauce and some of the tofu mix. Add another 2-3 noodles on top, then another layer of sauce, then another layer of tofu. Finish with a layer of noodles and a final layer of sauce. Sprinkle with mozzarella cheese on top.
4. Place the pan in the air fryer and Bake for 15 minutes or until the noodle edges are browned and the cheese is melted.
5. Cut and serve.
6. **Variations & Ingredients Tips**:
7. Substitute tofu with ricotta cheese for a more traditional lasagna.
8. Add sautéed mushrooms, zucchini, or bell peppers to the filling.
9. Use gluten-free lasagna noodles for a gluten-free version.
10. **Per Serving**: Calories: 420; Total Fat: 15g; Saturated Fat: 4g; Sodium: 720mg; Total Carbohydrates: 53g; Dietary Fiber: 6g; Total Sugars: 9g; Protein: 23g

Vegetable Side Dishes Recipes

Chicken Salad With Sunny Citrus Dressing

Servings: 4
Prep Time: 15 Minutes | Cooking Time: 8 Minutes
Ingredients:

- Sunny Citrus Dressing
- 1 cup first cold-pressed extra virgin olive oil
- ⅓ cup red wine vinegar
- 2 tablespoons all natural orange marmalade
- 1 teaspoon dry mustard
- 1 teaspoon ground black pepper
- California Chicken
- 4 large chicken tenders
- 1 teaspoon olive oil
- Juice of 1 small orange or clementine
- Salt and pepper
- ½ teaspoon rosemary
- Salad
- 8 cups romaine or leaf lettuce, chopped or torn into bite-size pieces
- 2 clementines or small oranges, peeled and sectioned
- ½ cup dried cranberries
- 4 tablespoons sliced almonds

Directions:

1. Make dressing: In a jar, combine all dressing ingredients and shake until blended. Refrigerate 30 mins.
2. Brush tenders with 1 tsp oil. Drizzle orange juice over them and season with salt, pepper, rosemary.
3. Cook at 198°C/390°F for 3 mins, turn over, cook 5 more mins until juices run clear.
4. To serve: Toss lettuce with 2 tbsp dressing. Divide among 4 plates.
5. Top with chicken, clementines, cranberries and almonds. Pass extra dressing.
6. **Variations & Ingredients Tips**:
7. Use spinach or arugula instead of romaine.
8. Add sliced avocado or cucumber.
9. Substitute honey mustard or balsamic vinaigrette for dressing.

10. **Per Serving**: Calories 545; Total Fat 37g; Saturated Fat 5g; Cholesterol 50mg; Sodium 220mg; Total Carbs 31g; Fiber 9g; Sugars 19g; Protein 27g

Broccoli Tots

Servings: 24 Tots
Prep Time: 10 Minutes | Cooking Time: 10 Minutes
Ingredients:

- 2 cups (225g) broccoli florets
- 1 egg, beaten
- ⅛ teaspoon onion powder
- ¼ teaspoon salt
- ⅛ teaspoon pepper
- 2 tablespoons grated Parmesan cheese
- ¼ cup panko breadcrumbs
- Oil for misting

Directions:

1. Steam broccoli for 2 minutes. Rinse in cold water, drain well, and chop finely.
2. In a large bowl, mix broccoli with all other ingredients except the oil.
3. Scoop out small portions of mixture and shape into 24 tots. Lay them on a cookie sheet or wax paper as you work.
4. Spray tots with oil and place in air fryer basket in single layer.
5. Cook at 198°C/390°F for 5 minutes. Shake basket and spray with oil again. Cook 5 minutes longer or until browned and crispy.
6. **Variations & Ingredients Tips**:
7. Substitute cauliflower for the broccoli.
8. Add shredded cheddar or feta to the mixture.
9. Serve with ranch, marinara or garlic aioli for dipping.
10. **Per Serving**: Calories 30; Total Fat 1g; Saturated Fat 0g; Cholesterol 15mg; Sodium 85mg; Total Carbs 4g; Fiber 1g; Sugars 0g; Protein 2g

Smoked Avocado Wedges

Servings: 4
Prep Time: 5 Minutes | Cooking Time: 15 Minutes
Ingredients:

- ½ teaspoon smoked paprika
- 2 teaspoons olive oil
- ½ lime, juiced
- 8 peeled avocado wedges
- 1 teaspoon chipotle powder
- ¼ teaspoon salt

Directions:

1. Preheat air fryer to 200°C/400°F.
2. Drizzle the avocado wedges with olive oil and lime juice.
3. In a bowl, combine chipotle powder, smoked paprika, and salt. Sprinkle over the avocado wedges.
4. Place them in the frying basket and Air Fry for 7 minutes.
5. Serve immediately.
6. **Variations & Ingredients Tips**:
7. Use lemon juice instead of lime juice for a different citrus flavor.
8. Add some chopped cilantro or parsley for a fresh herb flavor.
9. Serve the avocado wedges with salsa or guacamole for a Mexican-inspired side dish.
10. **Per Serving**: Calories: 130; Total Fat: 12g; Saturated Fat: 1.5g; Cholesterol: 0mg; Sodium: 150mg; Total Carbs: 6g; Fiber: 5g; Sugars: 0g; Protein: 1g

Brown Rice And Goat Cheese Croquettes

Servings: 3
Prep Time: 15 Minutes | Cooking Time: 8 Minutes
Ingredients:

- ¾ cup Water
- 6 tablespoons Raw medium-grain brown rice, such as brown Arborio
- ½ cup Shredded carrot
- ¼ cup Walnut pieces
- 3 tablespoons (about 43g) Soft goat cheese
- 1 tablespoon Pasteurized egg substitute, such as Egg Beaters (gluten-free, if a concern)
- ¼ teaspoon Dried thyme
- ¼ teaspoon Table salt
- ¼ teaspoon Ground black pepper
- Olive oil spray

Directions:

1. Combine the water, rice, and carrots in a small saucepan set over medium-high heat. Bring to a boil, stirring occasionally. Cover, reduce the heat to very low, and simmer very slowly for 45 minutes, or until the water has been absorbed and the rice is tender. Set aside, covered, for 10 minutes.
2. Scrape the contents of the saucepan into a food processor. Cool for 10 minutes.
3. Preheat the air fryer to 200°C/400°F.
4. Put the nuts, cheese, egg substitute, thyme, salt, and pepper into the food processor. Cover and pulse to a coarse paste, stopping the machine at least once to scrape down the inside of the canister.
5. Uncover the food processor; scrape down and remove the blade. Using wet, clean hands, form the mixture into two 10cm-diameter patties for a small batch, three 10cm-diameter patties for a medium batch, or four 10cm-diameter patties for a large one. Generously coat both sides of the patties with olive oil spray.
6. Set the patties in the basket with as much air space between them as possible. Air-fry undisturbed for 8 minutes, or until brown and crisp.
7. Use a nonstick-safe spatula to transfer the croquettes to a wire rack. Cool for 5 minutes before serving.
8. **Variations & Ingredients Tips**:
9. Substitute different grains like quinoa or farro for the brown rice.
10. Add finely chopped spinach or kale to the mixture.
11. Serve with a yogurt dill sauce for dipping.
12. **Per Serving**: Calories 225; Total Fat 10g; Saturated Fat 3g; Cholesterol 5mg; Sodium 330mg; Total Carbs 27g; Fiber 3g; Sugars 2g; Protein 8g

Crispy, Cheesy Leeks

Servings: 4
Prep Time: 10 Minutes | Cooking Time: 15 Minutes
Ingredients:

- 2 Medium leeks, about 255g each
- Olive oil spray
- ¼ cup Seasoned Italian-style dried bread crumbs (gluten-free, if a concern)
- ¼ cup (about 21g) Finely grated Parmesan cheese
- 2 tablespoons Olive oil

Directions:

1. Preheat air fryer to 177°C/350°F.

2. Trim leek ends, halve lengthwise. Remove inner layer halfway down. Coat all sides with olive oil spray.

3. Place leeks cut-side up in basket with space between pieces. Air fry 12 mins.

4. Meanwhile, mix breadcrumbs, cheese, and olive oil.

5. After 12 mins, sprinkle breadcrumb mixture over leeks. Increase to 190-198°C/375-390°F. Air fry 3 more mins until topping browns.

6. Transfer leeks to platter. Cool briefly before serving.

7. **Variations & Ingredients Tips**:

8. Add lemon zest and parsley to the breadcrumb mixture.

9. Use panko breadcrumbs for extra crunch.

10. Drizzle with balsamic glaze before serving.

11. **Per Serving**: Calories 130; Total Fat 9g; Saturated Fat 2g; Cholesterol 5mg; Sodium 160mg; Total Carbs 10g; Fiber 2g; Sugars 2g; Protein 3g

Acorn Squash Halves With Maple Butter Glaze

Servings: 2
Prep Time: 10 Minutes | Cooking Time: 33 Minutes
Ingredients:
- 1 medium (454g to 567g) Acorn squash
- Vegetable oil spray
- ¼ teaspoon Table salt
- 1½ tablespoons Butter, melted
- 1½ tablespoons Maple syrup

Directions:
1. Preheat the air fryer to 162°C/325°F (or 166°C/330°F, if that's the closest setting).

2. Cut a squash in half through the stem end. Use a flatware spoon (preferably, a serrated grapefruit spoon) to scrape out and discard the seeds and membranes in each half. Use a paring knife to make a crisscross pattern of cuts about 1.3 cm apart and 0.6 cm deep across the "meat" of the squash. If working with a second squash, repeat this step for that one.

3. Generously coat the cut side of the squash halves with vegetable oil spray. Sprinkle the halves with the salt. Set them in the basket cut side up with at least 0.6 cm between them. Air-fry undisturbed for 30 minutes.

4. Increase the machine's temperature to 204°C/400°F. Mix the melted butter and syrup in a small bowl until uniform. Brush this mixture over the cut sides of the squash(es), letting it pool in the center.

Air-fry undisturbed for 3 minutes, or until the glaze is bubbling.

5. Use a nonstick-safe spatula and kitchen tongs to transfer the squash halves cut side up to a wire rack. Cool for 5 to 10 minutes before serving.

6. **Variations & Ingredients Tips**:

7. Substitute brown sugar for the maple syrup for a different flavor profile.

8. Add chopped pecans or walnuts to the glaze for crunch.

9. Sprinkle with cinnamon or pumpkin pie spice before glazing.

10. **Per Serving**: Calories 207; Total Fat 9g; Saturated Fat 5g; Cholesterol 20mg; Sodium 230mg; Total Carbs 33g; Fiber 3g; Sugars 12g; Protein 2g

French Fries

Servings: 4
Prep Time: 10 Minutes | Cooking Time: 25 Minutes
Ingredients:
- 2 cups fresh potatoes
- 2 teaspoons oil
- ½ teaspoon salt

Dirctions:
1. Cut potatoes into 3cm-wide slices, then into 1.3cm sticks.

2. Rinse potato sticks and blot dry.

3. In a bowl, mix the potatoes, oil, and salt.

4. Pour into air fryer basket.

5. Cook at 198°C/390°F for 10 mins. Shake basket and cook 15 more mins until golden brown.

6. **Variations & Ingredients Tips**:

7. Toss with cajun seasoning or ranch before cooking.

8. Use sweet potato fries instead of russet.

9. Drizzle with truffle oil and parmesan after frying.

10. **Per Serving**: Calories 120; Total Fat 3g; Saturated Fat 0g; Cholesterol 0mg; Sodium 200mg; Total Carbs 22g; Fiber 2g; Sugars 1g; Protein 2g

Moroccan Cauliflower

Servings: 6
Prep Time: 10 Minutes | Cooking Time: 15 Minutes
Ingredients:
- 1 tablespoon curry powder
- 2 teaspoons smoked paprika
- 1/2 teaspoon ground cumin

- 1/2 teaspoon salt
- 1 head cauliflower, cut into bite-size pieces
- 1/4 cup red wine vinegar
- 2 tablespoons extra-virgin olive oil
- 2 tablespoons chopped parsley

Directions:
1. Preheat the air fryer to 188°C/370°F.
2. In a bowl, mix the curry powder, paprika, cumin, and salt. Add cauliflower and stir to coat.
3. Pour vinegar over top and continue stirring.
4. Place cauliflower into air fryer basket and drizzle with olive oil.
5. Cook for 5 minutes, toss, and cook 5 more minutes.
6. Raise temperature to 204°C/400°F and cook 4-6 more minutes until crispy.
7. **Variations & Ingredients Tips**:
8. Substitute lemon or lime juice for the vinegar.
9. Add a pinch of cayenne for extra heat.
10. Toss with mint or cilantro instead of parsley.
11. **Per Serving**: 71 Calories; 4g Total Fat; 1g Saturated Fat; 0mg Cholesterol; 229mg Sodium; 7g Total Carbs; 3g Fiber; 3g Sugars; 2g Protein

Perfect Broccolini

Servings: 4
Prep Time: 5 Minutes | Cooking Time: 15 Minutes
Ingredients:
- 454g broccolini
- Olive oil spray
- Coarse sea salt or kosher salt

Directions:
1. Preheat air fryer to 190°C/375°F.
2. Arrange broccolini on a cutting board and generously coat all over with olive oil spray.
3. When air fryer is preheated, pile broccolini into the basket spreading into an even layer.
4. Air fry for 5 minutes, tossing once, until leaves begin to brown and crisp. Watch carefully.
5. Transfer broccolini to a platter, spread out pieces and season with salt to taste.
6. **Variations & Ingredients Tips**:
7. Toss with lemon juice, garlic or red pepper flakes before cooking.
8. Drizzle with balsamic glaze or sprinkle parmesan after cooking.
9. Roast with cherry tomatoes or sliced mushrooms.

10. **Per Serving**: 36 Calories; 1g Total Fat; 0g Saturated Fat; 0mg Cholesterol; 38mg Sodium; 6g Total Carbs; 3g Fiber; 2g Sugars; 4g Protein

Panko-crusted Zucchini Fries

Servings: 6
Prep Time: 15 Minutes | Cooking Time: 8 Minutes
Ingredients:
- 3 medium zucchini
- 1/2 cup flour
- 1 teaspoon salt, divided
- 1/2 teaspoon black pepper, divided
- 3/4 teaspoon dried thyme, divided
- 2 large eggs
- 1 1/2 cups whole-wheat or plain panko breadcrumbs
- 1/2 cup grated Parmesan cheese

Directions:
1. Preheat the air fryer to 193°C/380°F.
2. Slice the zucchini into 1.25cm thick fry-like strips.
3. In a bowl, mix flour, 1/2 tsp salt, 1/4 tsp pepper, 1/2 tsp thyme.
4. In another bowl, whisk eggs, remaining 1/2 tsp salt, 1/4 tsp pepper.
5. In a third bowl, mix breadcrumbs, cheese, remaining 1/4 tsp thyme.
6. Dip zucchini in flour, then egg, then breadcrumb mixture to coat.
7. Arrange breaded fries in air fryer basket, spray with oil, and cook 4 mins.
8. Shake basket and cook 4-6 more mins until golden brown.
9. Serve warm.
10. **Variations & Ingredients Tips**:
11. Add parmesan or ranch seasoning to the breadcrumb mixture.
12. Use gluten-free breadcrumbs for a gluten-free version.
13. Serve with marinara, ranch or cheese sauce for dipping.
14. **Per Serving**: 156 Calories; 5g Total Fat; 2g Saturated Fat; 58mg Cholesterol; 500mg Sodium; 22g Total Carbs; 3g Fiber; 3g Sugars; 8g Protein

Balsamic Beet Chips

Servings: 4

Prep Time: 10 Minutes | Cooking Time: 40 Minutes

Ingredients:

- ½ tsp balsamic vinegar
- 4 beets, peeled and sliced
- 1 garlic clove, minced
- 2 tbsp chopped mint
- Salt and pepper to taste
- 3 tbsp olive oil

Directions:

1. Preheat air fryer to 193°C/380°F.
2. Coat all ingredients in a bowl, except balsamic vinegar.
3. Pour the beet mixture into the frying basket and Roast for 25-30 minutes, stirring once.
4. Serve, drizzled with vinegar and enjoy!
5. **Variations & Ingredients Tips**:
6. Use different fresh herbs like rosemary or thyme.
7. Toss with parmesan cheese before cooking.
8. Sprinkle with smoked paprika or cumin after cooking.
9. **Per Serving**: Calories 125; Total Fat 9g; Saturated Fat 1g; Cholesterol 0mg; Sodium 125mg; Total Carbs 10g; Fiber 2g; Sugars 8g; Protein 1g

Spiced Pumpkin Wedges

Servings: 4

Prep Time: 10 Minutes | Cooking Time: 35 Minutes

Ingredients:

- 625 ml pumpkin, cubed
- 2 tablespoons olive oil
- Salt and pepper to taste
- ¼ teaspoon pumpkin pie spice
- 1 tablespoon thyme
- 30 g grated Parmesan

Directions:

1. Preheat air fryer to 180°C/360°F.
2. Put the cubed pumpkin with olive oil, salt, pumpkin pie spice, black pepper, and thyme in a bowl and stir until the pumpkin is well coated.
3. Pour this mixture into the frying basket and Roast for 18-20 minutes, stirring once.
4. Sprinkle the pumpkin with grated Parmesan.
5. Serve and enjoy!
6. **Variations & Ingredients Tips**:

7. Use different types of winter squash, such as butternut squash or acorn squash, for a variety of flavors and textures.
8. Add some chopped pecans or walnuts for a crunchy texture and nutty flavor.
9. For a sweeter version, drizzle the pumpkin wedges with honey or maple syrup before serving.
10. **Per Serving**: Calories: 130; Total Fat: 8g; Saturated Fat: 2g; Cholesterol: 5mg; Sodium: 180mg; Total Carbs: 12g; Fiber: 2g; Sugars: 3g; Protein: 4g

Roasted Herbed Shiitake Mushrooms

Cooking Time: 5 Minutes

Prep Time: 5 Minutes | Servings: 4

Ingredients:

- 227g shiitake mushrooms, stemmed and caps chopped
- 1 tablespoon olive oil
- 1/2 teaspoon salt
- Freshly ground black pepper
- 1 teaspoon chopped fresh thyme
- 1 teaspoon chopped fresh oregano
- 1 tablespoon chopped fresh parsley

Directions:

1. Preheat air fryer to 204°C/400°F.
2. In a bowl, toss mushrooms with olive oil, salt, pepper, thyme and oregano.
3. Transfer mushrooms to air fryer basket and cook for 5 minutes, shaking basket 1-2 times.
4. For more tender mushrooms, increase cook time by 2 minutes.
5. Once cooked, toss mushrooms with chopped parsley.
6. Season again to taste and serve.
7. **Variations & Ingredients Tips**:
8. Use a blend of wild mushroom varieties.
9. Add minced garlic or shallots before roasting.
10. Finish with a squeeze of lemon juice.
11. **Per Serving**: 55 Calories; 4g Total Fat; 1g Saturated Fat; 0mg Cholesterol; 234mg Sodium; 4g Total Carbs; 1g Fiber; 2g Sugars; 2g Protein

Hasselbacks

Servings: 4

Prep Time: 10 Minutes | Cooking Time: 41 Minutes

Ingredients:

- 2 large (454g each) potatoes
- Oil for misting or cooking spray
- Salt, pepper, and garlic powder
- 43g sharp cheddar cheese, sliced very thin
- 1/4 cup chopped green onions
- 2 strips turkey bacon, cooked and crumbled
- Light sour cream for serving (optional)

Directions:

1. Preheat air fryer to 199°C/390°F.
2. Scrub potatoes. Cut thin vertical slices 6mm thick crosswise about three-quarters of the way down so that bottom of potato remains intact.
3. Fan potatoes slightly to separate slices. Mist with oil and sprinkle with salt, pepper, and garlic powder to taste.
4. Place potatoes in air fryer basket and cook for 40 minutes or until centers test done when pierced with a fork.
5. Top potatoes with cheese slices and cook for 30 seconds to 1 minute to melt cheese.
6. Cut each potato in half crosswise, and sprinkle with green onions and crumbled bacon. If desired, add a dollop of sour cream before serving.
7. **Variations & Ingredients Tips**:
8. Mix shredded cheese into the seasoning before baking for extra cheesy potatoes.
9. Brush with garlic butter before serving.
10. Top with chives, bacon bits, sour cream or salsa.
11. **Per Serving**: 292 Calories; 9g Total Fat; 4g Saturated Fat; 21mg Cholesterol; 283mg Sodium; 46g Total Carbs; 4g Fiber; 3g Sugars; 10g Protein

Balsamic Green Beans With Bacon

Servings: 4
Prep Time: 5 Minutes | Cooking Time: 15 Minutes
Ingredients:

- 2 cups green beans, trimmed
- 1 tbsp butter, melted
- Salt and pepper to taste
- 1 bacon slice, diced
- 1 clove garlic, minced
- 1 tbsp balsamic vinegar

Directions:

1. Preheat air fryer to 190°C/375°F.
2. Combine green beans, butter, salt, and pepper in a bowl.
3. Put the bean mixture in the frying basket and Air Fry for 5 minutes.
4. Stir in bacon and Air Fry for 4 more minutes.
5. Mix in garlic and cook for 1 minute.
6. Transfer it to a serving dish, drizzle with balsamic vinegar and combine.
7. Serve right away.
8. **Variations & Ingredients Tips**:
9. Substitute pancetta or prosciutto for the bacon.
10. Toss with grated parmesan before serving.
11. Add sliced shallots or red pepper flakes for extra flavor.
12. **Per Serving**: Calories 80; Total Fat 4g; Saturated Fat 2g; Cholesterol 10mg; Sodium 115mg; Total Carbs 9g; Fiber 3g; Sugars 5g; Protein 3g

Five-spice Roasted Sweet Potatoes

Servings: 4
Prep Time: 10 Minutes | Cooking Time: 12 Minutes
Ingredients:

- ½ teaspoon ground cinnamon
- ¼ teaspoon ground cumin
- ¼ teaspoon paprika
- 1 teaspoon chile powder
- ⅛ teaspoon turmeric
- ½ teaspoon salt (optional)
- Freshly ground black pepper
- 2 large sweet potatoes, peeled and cut into 2cm cubes (about 3 cups)
- 1 tablespoon olive oil

Directions:

1. In a large bowl, mix together cinnamon, cumin, paprika, chile powder, turmeric, salt, and pepper to taste.
2. Add potatoes and stir well.
3. Drizzle the seasoned potatoes with olive oil and stir until evenly coated.
4. Place seasoned potatoes in the air fryer baking pan or dish that fits basket.
5. Cook for 6 minutes at 198°C/390°F, stop and stir well.

6. Cook for an additional 6 minutes.
7. **Variations & Ingredients Tips**:
8. Add a pinch of cayenne for extra heat.
9. Toss with maple syrup before cooking.
10. Sprinkle with sliced green onions after roasting.
11. **Per Serving**: Calories 150; Total Fat 4g; Saturated Fat 1g; Cholesterol 0mg; Sodium 200mg; Total Carbs 26g; Fiber 4g; Sugars 7g; Protein 2g

Fried Eggplant Slices

Servings: 3
Prep Time: 15 Minutes | Cooking Time: 12 Minutes
Ingredients:
- 1½ sleeves (about 90 crackers) Saltine crackers
- ¾ cup Cornstarch
- 2 Large eggs, well beaten
- 1 medium (about 340g) Eggplant, stemmed, peeled, cut into 6mm slices
- Olive oil spray

Directions:
1. Preheat air fryer to 200°C/400°F. Position oven rack in center and heat oven to 75°C/175°F.
2. Grind crackers in batches in a food processor into small bits, not crumbs.
3. Set up 3 shallow dishes: 1 with cornstarch, 1 with beaten eggs, 1 with crushed crackers.
4. Coat eggplant slices in cornstarch, dip in egg, then coat in cracker crumbs. Spray both sides with oil.
5. Place 1-3 slices in air fryer basket with space between. Air fry 12 mins until crisp.
6. Transfer to baking sheet and keep warm in oven as you fry batches.
7. **Variations & Ingredients Tips**:
8. Use panko breadcrumbs instead of saltines.
9. Add grated parmesan or Italian seasoning to the crumb coating.
10. Serve with marinara sauce for dipping.
11. **Per Serving**: Calories 250; Total Fat 6g; Saturated Fat 1g; Cholesterol 110mg; Sodium 510mg; Total Carbs 43g; Fiber 5g; Sugars 3g; Protein 8g

Rich Baked Sweet Potatoes

Servings: 2
Prep Time: 5 Minutes | Cooking Time: 55 Minutes
Ingredients:
- 454g sweet potatoes, scrubbed and perforated with a fork
- 2 tsp olive oil
- Salt and pepper to taste
- 2 tbsp butter
- 3 tbsp honey

Directions:
1. Preheat air fryer at 204°C/400°F.
2. Mix olive oil, salt, pepper and honey in a bowl.
3. Brush the sweet potatoes all over with the honey oil mixture.
4. Place sweet potatoes in the air fryer basket and bake for 45 minutes, turning over halfway.
5. Let cool 10 minutes until cool enough to handle.
6. Slice each potato lengthwise and press ends together to open up slices.
7. Top with butter before serving.
8. **Variations & Ingredients Tips**:
9. Add cinnamon, nutmeg or pumpkin spice to the honey oil mixture.
10. Stuff baked sweet potatoes with sauteed spinach or black beans.
11. Top with pecans, marshmallows or brown sugar before serving.
12. **Per Serving**: 291 Calories; 11g Total Fat; 4g Saturated Fat; 15mg Cholesterol; 115mg Sodium; 48g Total Carbs; 5g Fiber; 23g Sugars; 2g Protein

Sea Salt Radishes

Servings: 4
Prep Time: 5 Minutes | Cooking Time: 25 Minutes
Ingredients:
- 454g radishes
- 2 tbsp olive oil
- 1/2 tsp sea salt
- 1/2 tsp garlic powder

Directions:
1. Preheat air fryer to 182°C/360°F.
2. In a bowl, toss the radishes with olive oil, garlic powder and sea salt until evenly coated.
3. Transfer radishes to the air fryer basket in a single layer.
4. Air fry for 18 minutes, tossing or shaking the basket halfway through cooking.
5. Serve hot.
6. **Variations & Ingredients Tips**:

7. Use a variety of radish colors like red, white and purple.

8. Substitute ranch seasoning or Cajun spice blend for the garlic powder.

9. Drizzle with a bit of fresh lemon juice before serving.

10. **Per Serving**: 68 Calories; 5g Total Fat; 1g Saturated Fat; omg Cholesterol; 193mg Sodium; 5g Total Carbs; 2g Fiber; 3g Sugars; 1g Protein

General Tso's Cauliflower

Servings: 3

Prep Time: 10 Minutes | Cooking Time: 15 Minutes

Ingredients:

- ⅓ cup All-purpose flour or tapioca flour
- 2 Large eggs, well beaten
- ⅔ cup Plain panko breadcrumbs
- 2½ cups (about 340g) 3.8cm cauliflower florets
- Vegetable oil spray
- Sauce:
- 2 tablespoons Regular or low-sodium soy sauce or gluten-free tamari
- 1 tablespoon Hoisin sauce
- 1 tablespoon Unseasoned rice vinegar
- 2 teaspoons Granulated white sugar
- 1½ teaspoons Sriracha or hot sauce
- Water and cornstarch if needed for thickening

Directions:

1. Preheat air fryer to 200°C/400°F.

2. Put flour in one bag, beaten eggs in second, breadcrumbs in third.

3. Coat cauliflower in flour, then egg, then breadcrumbs - transferring between bags.

4. Arrange breaded florets on paper towels and spray all over with oil.

5. Air fry in a single layer for 15 mins until crisp.

6. Make sauce: Simmer soy sauce, hoisin, vinegar, sugar and sriracha.

7. If needed, mix water and cornstarch, whisk into sauce to thicken. Remove from heat.

8. Toss cooked cauliflower in sauce to coat. Serve warm.

9. **Variations & Ingredients Tips**:

10. Use plant-based eggs and panko for a vegan version.

11. Add garlic, ginger or scallions to the sauce.

12. Toss in orange or pineapple chunks at the end.

13. **Per Serving**: Calories 230; Total Fat 6g; Saturated Fat 1g; Cholesterol 105mg; Sodium 640mg; Total Carbs 35g; Fiber 2g; Sugars 8g; Protein 8g

Sandwiches And Burgers Recipes

Chili Cheese Dogs

Servings: 3
Prep Time: 10 Minutes | Cooking Time: 12 Minutes
Ingredients:

- 340 grams Lean ground beef
- 1½ tablespoons Chile powder
- 240 grams plus 2 tablespoons Jarred sofrito
- 3 Hot dogs (gluten-free, if a concern)
- 3 Hot dog buns (gluten-free, if a concern), split open lengthwise
- 3 tablespoons Finely chopped scallion
- 60 grams Shredded Cheddar cheese

Directions:

1. Crumble the ground beef into a medium or large saucepan set over medium heat. Brown well, stirring often to break up the clumps. Add the chile powder and cook for 30 seconds, stirring the whole time. Stir in the sofrito and bring to a simmer. Reduce the heat to low and simmer, stirring occasionally, for 5 minutes. Keep warm.

2. Preheat the air fryer to 200℃/400°F.

3. When the machine is at temperature, put the hot dogs in the basket and air-fry undisturbed for 10 minutes, or until the hot dogs are bubbling and blistered, even a little crisp.

4. Use kitchen tongs to put the hot dogs in the buns. Top each with about 120 grams of the ground beef mixture, 1 tablespoon of the minced scallion, and 20 grams of the cheese. (The scallion should go under the cheese so it superheats and wilts a bit.) Set the filled hot dog buns in the basket and air-fry undisturbed for 2 minutes, or until the cheese has melted.

5. Remove the basket from the machine. Cool the chili cheese dogs in the basket for 5 minutes before serving.

6. **Variations & Ingredients Tips:**

7. Use turkey or veggie hot dogs for a healthier option.

8. Substitute cheddar cheese with your favorite melty cheese, such as pepper jack or Swiss.

9. Add diced onions or jalapeños to the chili for extra flavor and heat.

10. **Per Serving**: Calories: 580; Cholesterol: 110mg; Total Fat: 32g; Saturated Fat: 13g; Sodium: 1420mg; Total Carbohydrates: 36g; Dietary Fiber: 5g; Total Sugars: 6g; Protein: 38g

Reuben Sandwiches

Servings: 2
Prep Time: 10 Minutes | Cooking Time: 11 Minutes
Ingredients:

- 225 grams Sliced deli corned beef
- 4 teaspoons Regular or low-fat mayonnaise (not fat-free)
- 4 Rye bread slices
- 2 tablespoons plus 2 teaspoons Russian dressing
- ½ cup Purchased sauerkraut, squeezed by the handful over the sink to get rid of excess moisture
- 55 grams (2 to 4 slices) Swiss cheese slices (optional)

Directions:

1. Set the corned beef in the basket, slip the basket into the machine, and heat the air fryer to 200℃/400°F. Air-fry undisturbed for 3 minutes from the time the basket is put in the machine, just to warm up the meat.

2. Use kitchen tongs to transfer the corned beef to a cutting board. Spread 1 teaspoon mayonnaise on one side of each slice of rye bread, rubbing the mayonnaise into the bread with a small flatware knife.

3. Place the bread slices mayonnaise side down on a cutting board. Spread the Russian dressing over the "dry" side of each slice. For one sandwich, top one slice of bread with the corned beef, sauerkraut, and cheese (if using). For two sandwiches, top two slices of bread each with half of the corned beef, sauerkraut, and cheese (if using). Close the sandwiches with the remaining bread, setting it mayonnaise side up on top.

4. Set the sandwich(es) in the basket and air-fry undisturbed for 8 minutes, or until browned and crunchy.

5. Use a nonstick-safe spatula, and perhaps a flatware fork for balance, to transfer the sandwich(es) to a cutting board. Cool for 2 or 3 minutes before slicing in half and serving.

6. **Variations & Ingredients Tips:**

7. Substitute corned beef with pastrami for a classic New York deli taste.

8. Use Thousand Island dressing instead of Russian dressing for a tangy, sweet flavor.

9. Add sliced dill pickles or mustard to the sandwich for extra zing.

10. **Per Serving** (1 sandwich): Calories: 520; Cholesterol: 75mg; Total Fat: 30g; Saturated Fat: 9g; Sodium: 2020mg; Total Carbohydrates: 36g; Dietary Fiber: 4g; Total Sugars: 6g; Protein: 29g

White Bean Veggie Burgers

Servings: 3

Prep Time: 15 Minutes | Cooking Time: 13 Minutes

Ingredients:

- 320 grams Drained and rinsed canned white beans
- 3 tablespoons Rolled oats (not quick-cooking or steel-cut; gluten-free, if a concern)
- 3 tablespoons Chopped walnuts
- 2 teaspoons Olive oil
- 2 teaspoons Lemon juice
- 1½ teaspoons Dijon mustard (gluten-free, if a concern)
- ¾ teaspoon Dried sage leaves
- ¼ teaspoon Table salt
- Olive oil spray
- 3 Whole-wheat buns or gluten-free whole-grain buns (if a concern), split open

Directions:

1. Preheat the air fryer to 200℃/400°F.

2. Place the beans, oats, walnuts, oil, lemon juice, mustard, sage, and salt in a food processor. Cover and process to make a coarse paste that will hold its shape, about like wet sugar-cookie dough, stopping the machine to scrape down the inside of the canister at least once.

3. Scrape down and remove the blade. With clean and wet hands, form the bean paste into two 10-cm patties for the small batch, three 10-cm patties for the medium, or four 10-cm patties for the large batch. Generously coat the patties on both sides with olive oil spray.

4. Set them in the basket with some space between them and air-fry undisturbed for 12 minutes, or until lightly brown and crisp at the edges. The tops of the burgers will feel firm to the touch.

5. Use a nonstick-safe spatula, and perhaps a flatware fork for balance, to transfer the burgers to a cutting board. Set the buns cut side down in the basket in one layer (working in batches as necessary) and air-fry undisturbed for 1 minute, to toast a bit and warm up. Serve the burgers warm in the buns.

6. **Variations & Ingredients Tips**:

7. Use black beans, chickpeas, or lentils instead of white beans for a different flavor and color.

8. Add grated carrots, zucchini, or beets to the burger mixture for extra nutrition and texture.

9. Serve with your favorite burger toppings like lettuce, tomato, onion, and pickles.

10. **Per Serving** (1 burger): Calories: 350; Cholesterol: 0mg; Total Fat: 13g; Saturated Fat: 1g; Sodium: 520mg; Total Carbohydrates: 48g; Dietary Fiber: 9g; Total Sugars: 4g; Protein: 14g

Perfect Burgers

Servings: 3

Prep Time: 10 Minutes | Cooking Time: 13 Minutes

Ingredients:

- 510 grams 90% lean ground beef
- 1½ tablespoons Worcestershire sauce (gluten-free, if a concern)
- ½ teaspoon Ground black pepper
- 3 Hamburger buns (gluten-free if a concern), split open

Directions:

1. Preheat the air fryer to 190℃/375°F.

2. Gently mix the ground beef, Worcestershire sauce, and pepper in a bowl until well combined but preserving as much of the meat's fibers as possible. Divide this mixture into two 15-cm patties for the small batch, three 12.5-cm patties for the medium, or four 12.5-cm patties for the large. Make a thumbprint indentation in the center of each patty, about halfway through the meat.

3. Set the patties in the basket in one layer with some space between them. Air-fry undisturbed for 10 minutes, or until an instant-read meat thermometer inserted into the center of a burger registers 70℃/160°F (a medium-well burger). You may need to add 2 minutes cooking time if the air fryer is at 180℃/360°F.

4. Use a nonstick-safe spatula, and perhaps a flatware fork for balance, to transfer the burgers to a cutting board. Set the buns cut side down in the basket in one layer (working in batches as necessary) and air-fry undisturbed for 1 minute, to toast a bit and warm up. Serve the burgers in the warm buns.

5. **Variations & Ingredients Tips**:

6. Mix in finely chopped onions, garlic, or herbs to the burger mixture for extra flavor.

7. Use a mixture of ground beef and ground pork or lamb for a juicier, more flavorful burger.

8. Top burgers with your favorite cheese, bacon, avocado, or sautéed mushrooms.

9. **Per Serving** (1 burger): Calories: 420; Cholesterol: 105mg; Total Fat: 22g; Saturated Fat: 8g; Sodium: 460mg; Total Carbohydrates: 23g; Dietary Fiber: 1g; Total Sugars: 3g; Protein: 34g

Philly Cheesesteak Sandwiches

Servings: 3
Prep Time: 10 Minutes | Cooking Time: 9 Minutes
Ingredients:

- 340 grams Shaved beef
- 1 tablespoon Worcestershire sauce (gluten-free, if a concern)
- ¼ teaspoon Garlic powder
- ¼ teaspoon Mild paprika
- 6 tablespoons (45 grams) Frozen bell pepper strips (do not thaw)
- 2 slices, broken into rings Very thin yellow or white medium onion slice(s)
- 170 grams (6 to 8 slices) Provolone cheese slices
- 3 Long soft rolls such as hero, hoagie, or Italian sub rolls, or hot dog buns (gluten-free, if a concern), split open lengthwise

Directions:

1. Preheat the air fryer to 200℃/400°F.

2. When the machine is at temperature, spread the shaved beef in the basket, leaving a 1.25-cm perimeter around the meat for good air flow. Sprinkle the meat with the Worcestershire sauce, paprika, and garlic powder. Spread the peppers and onions on top of the meat.

3. Air-fry undisturbed for 6 minutes, or until cooked through. Set the cheese on top of the meat. Continue air-frying undisturbed for 3 minutes, or until the cheese has melted.

4. Use kitchen tongs to divide the meat and cheese layers in the basket between the rolls or buns. Serve hot.

5. **Variations & Ingredients Tips**:

6. Use thinly sliced ribeye or sirloin steak instead of shaved beef for a more traditional texture.

7. Add sliced mushrooms to the pepper and onion mixture for extra flavor and nutrition.

8. Substitute provolone with American cheese or Cheez Whiz for a classic Philly taste.

9. **Per Serving**: Calories: 620; Cholesterol: 135mg; Total Fat: 32g; Saturated Fat: 15g; Sodium: 1320mg; Total Carbohydrates: 38g; Dietary Fiber: 2g; Total Sugars: 5g; Protein: 48g

Crunchy Falafel Balls

Servings: 8
Prep Time: 15 Minutes | Cooking Time: 16 Minutes
Ingredients:

- 600 grams Drained and rinsed canned chickpeas
- 60 grams Olive oil
- 3 tablespoons All-purpose flour
- 1½ teaspoons Dried oregano
- 1½ teaspoons Dried sage leaves
- 1½ teaspoons Dried thyme
- ¾ teaspoon Table salt
- Olive oil spray

Directions:

1. Preheat the air fryer to 200℃/400°F.

2. Place the chickpeas, olive oil, flour, oregano, sage, thyme, and salt in a food processor. Cover and process into a paste, stopping the machine at least once to scrape down the inside of the canister.

3. Scrape down and remove the blade. Using clean, wet hands, form 2 tablespoons of the paste into a ball, then continue making 9 more balls for a small batch, 15 more for a medium one, and 19 more for a large batch. Generously coat the balls in olive oil spray.

4. Set the balls in the basket in one layer with a little space between them and air-fry undisturbed for 16 minutes, or until well browned and crisp.

5. Dump the contents of the basket onto a wire rack. Cool for 5 minutes before serving.

6. **Variations & Ingredients Tips**:

7. Add minced garlic, onion, or herbs like parsley or cilantro for extra flavor.

8. Serve with tahini sauce, hummus, or tzatziki for dipping.

9. Make a falafel sandwich by stuffing pita bread with falafel balls, lettuce, tomato, and sauce.

10. **Per Serving** (2 falafel balls): Calories: 170; Cholesterol: 0mg; Total Fat: 9g; Saturated Fat: 1g;

Sodium: 230mg; Total Carbohydrates: 18g; Dietary Fiber: 4g; Total Sugars: 2g; Protein: 5g

Total Carbohydrates: 41g; Dietary Fiber: 2g; Total Sugars: 6g; Protein: 45g

Chicken Apple Brie Melt

Servings: 3
Prep Time: 10 Minutes | Cooking Time: 13 Minutes
Ingredients:

- 3 140 to 170-gram boneless skinless chicken breasts
- Vegetable oil spray
- 1½ teaspoons Dried herbes de Provence
- 85 grams Brie, rind removed, thinly sliced
- 6 Thin cored apple slices
- 3 French rolls (gluten-free, if a concern)
- 2 tablespoons Dijon mustard (gluten-free, if a concern)

Directions:

1. Preheat the air fryer to 190℃/375°F.
2. Lightly coat all sides of the chicken breasts with vegetable oil spray. Sprinkle the breasts evenly with the herbes de Provence.
3. When the machine is at temperature, set the breasts in the basket and air-fry undisturbed for 10 minutes.
4. Top the chicken breasts with the apple slices, then the cheese. Air-fry undisturbed for 2 minutes, or until the cheese is melty and bubbling.
5. Use a nonstick-safe spatula and kitchen tongs, for balance, to transfer the breasts to a cutting board. Set the rolls in the basket and air-fry for 1 minute to warm through. (Putting them in the machine without splitting them keeps the insides very soft while the outside gets a little crunchy.)
6. Transfer the rolls to the cutting board. Split them open lengthwise, then spread 1 teaspoon mustard on each cut side. Set a prepared chicken breast on the bottom of a roll and close with its top, repeating as necessary to make additional sandwiches. Serve warm.
7. **Variations & Ingredients Tips**:
8. Substitute the Brie with Camembert or another soft cheese of your choice.
9. Use pears instead of apples for a different flavor profile.
10. Add baby spinach or arugula for extra greens and nutrition.
11. **Per Serving**: Calories: 510; Cholesterol: 135mg; Total Fat: 19g; Saturated Fat: 8g; Sodium: 670mg;

Sausage And Pepper Heros

Servings: 3
Prep Time: 10 Minutes | Cooking Time: 11 Minutes
Ingredients:

- 3 links (about 255 grams total) Sweet Italian sausages (gluten-free, if a concern)
- 1½ Medium red or green bell pepper(s), stemmed, cored, and cut into 1.25-cm-wide strips
- 1 medium Yellow or white onion(s), peeled, halved, and sliced into thin half-moons
- 3 Long soft rolls, such as hero, hoagie, or Italian sub rolls (gluten-free, if a concern), split open lengthwise
- For garnishing Balsamic vinegar
- For garnishing Fresh basil leaves

Directions:

1. Preheat the air fryer to 200℃/400°F.
2. When the machine is at temperature, set the sausage links in the basket in one layer and air-fry undisturbed for 5 minutes.
3. Add the pepper strips and onions. Continue air-frying, tossing and rearranging everything about once every minute, for 5 minutes, or until the sausages are browned and an instant-read meat thermometer inserted into one of the links registers 70℃/160°F.
4. Use a nonstick-safe spatula and kitchen tongs to transfer the sausages and vegetables to a cutting board. Set the rolls cut side down in the basket in one layer (working in batches as necessary) and air-fry undisturbed for 1 minute, to toast the rolls a bit and warm them up. Set 1 sausage with some pepper strips and onions in each warm roll, sprinkle balsamic vinegar over the sandwich fillings, and garnish with basil leaves.
5. **Variations & Ingredients Tips**:
6. Use hot Italian sausage or chorizo for a spicier sandwich.
7. Add sliced mushrooms or zucchini to the pepper and onion mixture for extra veggies.
8. Top with shredded mozzarella or provolone cheese for a cheesy twist.
9. **Per Serving** (1 sandwich): Calories: 560; Cholesterol: 60mg; Total Fat: 36g; Saturated Fat: 12g;

Sodium: 1420mg; Total Carbohydrates: 39g; Dietary Fiber: 3g; Total Sugars: 7g; Protein: 24g

Best-ever Roast Beef Sandwiches

Servings: 6

Prep Time: 10 Minutes | Cooking Time: 30-50 Minutes

Ingredients:

- 2½ teaspoons Olive oil
- 1½ teaspoons Dried oregano
- 1½ teaspoons Dried thyme
- 1½ teaspoons Onion powder
- 1½ teaspoons Table salt
- 1½ teaspoons Ground black pepper
- 1 kg Beef eye of round
- 6 Round soft rolls, such as Kaiser rolls or hamburger buns (gluten-free, if a concern), split open lengthwise
- ¾ cup Regular, low-fat, or fat-free mayonnaise (gluten-free, if a concern)
- 6 Romaine lettuce leaves, rinsed
- 6 Round tomato slices (0.5 cm thick)

Directions:

1. Preheat the air fryer to 180℃/350°F.

2. Mix the oil, oregano, thyme, onion powder, salt, and pepper in a small bowl. Spread this mixture all over the eye of round.

3. When the machine is at temperature, set the beef in the basket and air-fry for 30 to 50 minutes (the range depends on the size of the cut), turning the meat twice, until an instant-read meat thermometer inserted into the thickest piece of the meat registers 55℃/130°F for rare, 60℃/140°F for medium, or 65℃/150°F for well-done.

4. Use kitchen tongs to transfer the beef to a cutting board. Cool for 10 minutes. If serving now, carve into 3-mm-thick slices. Spread each roll with 2 tablespoons mayonnaise and divide the beef slices between the rolls. Top with a lettuce leaf and a tomato slice and serve. Or set the beef in a container, cover, and refrigerate for up to 3 days to make cold roast beef sandwiches anytime.

5. **Variations & Ingredients Tips**:

6. Experiment with different herbs and spices in the rub, such as garlic powder, paprika, or rosemary.

7. Add sliced red onions or pickles for extra flavor and crunch.

8. Use leftover roast beef for cold sandwiches or salads.

9. **Per Serving**: Calories: 560; Cholesterol: 115mg; Total Fat: 27g; Saturated Fat: 6g; Sodium: 980mg; Total Carbohydrates: 32g; Dietary Fiber: 2g; Total Sugars: 4g; Protein: 47g

Chicken Saltimbocca Sandwiches

Servings: 3

Prep Time: 10 Minutes | Cooking Time: 11 Minutes

Ingredients:

- 3 140to 170-gram boneless skinless chicken breasts
- 6 Thin prosciutto slices
- 6 Provolone cheese slices
- 3 Long soft rolls, such as hero, hoagie, or Italian sub rolls (gluten-free, if a concern), split open lengthwise
- 3 tablespoons Pesto, purchased or homemade (see the headnote)

Directions:

1. Preheat the air fryer to 200℃/400°F.

2. Wrap each chicken breast with 2 prosciutto slices, spiraling the prosciutto around the breast and overlapping the slices a bit to cover the breast. The prosciutto will stick to the chicken more readily than bacon does.

3. When the machine is at temperature, set the wrapped chicken breasts in the basket and air-fry undisturbed for 10 minutes, or until the prosciutto is frizzled and the chicken is cooked through.

4. Overlap 2 cheese slices on each breast. Air-fry undisturbed for 1 minute, or until melted. Take the basket out of the machine.

5. Smear the insides of the rolls with the pesto, then use kitchen tongs to put a wrapped and cheesy chicken breast in each roll.

6. **Variations & Ingredients Tips**:

7. Use fresh mozzarella instead of provolone for a creamier texture.

8. Add sliced tomatoes or roasted red peppers for extra flavor and nutrition.

9. Substitute prosciutto with ham or bacon if desired.

10. **Per Serving**: Calories: 630; Cholesterol: 125mg; Total Fat: 32g; Saturated Fat: 11g; Sodium: 1580mg; Total Carbohydrates: 38g; Dietary Fiber: 2g; Total Sugars: 4g; Protein: 48g

Thai-style Pork Sliders

Servings: 4
Prep Time: 15 Minutes | Cooking Time: 15 Minutes
Ingredients:

- 310 grams Ground pork
- 2½ tablespoons Very thinly sliced scallions, white and green parts
- 4 teaspoons Minced peeled fresh ginger
- 2½ teaspoons Fish sauce (gluten-free, if a concern)
- 2 teaspoons Thai curry paste (see the headnote; gluten-free, if a concern)
- 2 teaspoons Light brown sugar
- ¾ teaspoon Ground black pepper
- 4 Slider buns (gluten-free, if a concern)

Directions:

1. Preheat the air fryer to 190℃/375°F.

2. Gently mix the pork, scallions, ginger, fish sauce, curry paste, brown sugar, and black pepper in a bowl until well combined. With clean, wet hands, form about 80 grams of the pork mixture into a slider about 6.5-cm in diameter. Repeat until you use up all the meat—3 sliders for the small batch, 4 for the medium, and 6 for the large. (Keep wetting your hands to help the patties adhere.)

3. When the machine is at temperature, set the sliders in the basket in one layer. Air-fry undisturbed for 14 minutes, or until the sliders are golden brown and caramelized at their edges and an instant-read meat thermometer inserted into the center of a slider registers 70℃/160°F.

4. Use a nonstick-safe spatula, and perhaps a flatware fork for balance, to transfer the sliders to a cutting board. Set the buns cut side down in the basket in one layer (working in batches as necessary) and air-fry undisturbed for 1 minute, to toast a bit and warm up. Serve the sliders warm in the buns.

5. **Variations & Ingredients Tips**:

6. Use ground chicken or turkey for a leaner slider option.

7. Substitute Thai curry paste with red curry paste or green curry paste for a different flavor profile.

8. Serve with pickled vegetables, cilantro, and sriracha mayonnaise for extra Thai-inspired toppings.

9. **Per Serving** (1 slider): Calories: 240; Cholesterol: 65mg; Total Fat: 13g; Saturated Fat: 4g; Sodium:

Thanksgiving Turkey Sandwiches

Servings: 3
Prep Time: 15 Minutes | Cooking Time: 10 Minutes
Ingredients:

- 1½ cups Herb-seasoned stuffing mix (not cornbread-style; gluten-free, if a concern)
- 1 Large egg white(s)
- 2 tablespoons Water
- 3 140- to 170-gram turkey breast cutlets
- Vegetable oil spray
- 4½ tablespoons Purchased cranberry sauce, preferably whole berry
- ⅛ teaspoon Ground cinnamon
- ⅛ teaspoon Ground dried ginger
- 4½ tablespoons Regular, low-fat, or fat-free mayonnaise (gluten-free, if a concern)
- 6 tablespoons Shredded Brussels sprouts
- 3 Kaiser rolls (gluten-free, if a concern), split open

Directions:

1. Preheat the air fryer to 190℃/375°F.

2. Put the stuffing mix in a heavy zip-closed bag, seal it, lay it flat on your counter, and roll a rolling pin over the bag to crush the stuffing mix to the consistency of rough sand. (Or you can pulse the stuffing mix to the desired consistency in a food processor.)

3. Set up and fill two shallow soup plates or small pie plates on your counter: one for the egg white(s), whisked with the water until foamy; and one for the ground stuffing mix.

4. Dip a cutlet in the egg white mixture, coating both sides and letting any excess egg white slip back into the rest. Set the cutlet in the ground stuffing mix and coat it evenly on both sides, pressing gently to coat well on both sides. Lightly coat the cutlet on both sides with vegetable oil spray, set it aside, and continue dipping and coating the remaining cutlets in the same way.

5. Set the cutlets in the basket and air-fry undisturbed for 10 minutes, or until crisp and brown. Use kitchen tongs to transfer the cutlets to a wire rack to cool for a few minutes.

6. Meanwhile, stir the cranberry sauce with the cinnamon and ginger in a small bowl. Mix the

shredded Brussels sprouts and mayonnaise in a second bowl until the vegetable is evenly coated.

7. Build the sandwiches by spreading about 1½ tablespoons of the cranberry mixture on the cut side of the bottom half of each roll. Set a cutlet on top, then spread about 3 tablespoons of the Brussels sprouts mixture evenly over the cutlet. Set the other half of the roll on top and serve warm.

8. **Variations & Ingredients Tips**:

9. Use leftover roasted turkey instead of turkey cutlets for a post-Thanksgiving sandwich.

10. Substitute Brussels sprouts with shredded cabbage or kale for a different texture and flavor.

11. Add a slice of brie or provolone cheese to the sandwich for extra creaminess.

12. **Per Serving**: Calories: 530; Cholesterol: 75mg; Total Fat: 22g; Saturated Fat: 4g; Sodium: 1180mg; Total Carbohydrates: 53g; Dietary Fiber: 4g; Total Sugars: 15g; Protein: 33g

Chicken Club Sandwiches

Servings: 3
Prep Time: 15 Minutes | Cooking Time: 15 Minutes
Ingredients:

- 3 140- to 170-gram boneless skinless chicken breasts
- 6 Thick-cut bacon strips (gluten-free, if a concern)
- 3 Long soft rolls, such as hero, hoagie, or Italian sub rolls (gluten-free, if a concern)
- 3 tablespoons Regular, low-fat, or fat-free mayonnaise (gluten-free, if a concern)
- 3 Lettuce leaves, preferably romaine or iceberg
- 6 6-mm-thick tomato slices

Directions:

1. Preheat the air fryer to 190℃/375°F.

2. Wrap each chicken breast with 2 strips of bacon, spiraling the bacon around the meat, slightly overlapping the strips on each revolution. Start the second strip of bacon farther down the breast but on a line with the start of the first strip so they both end at a lined-up point on the chicken breast.

3. When the machine is at temperature, set the wrapped breasts bacon-seam side down in the basket with space between them. Air-fry undisturbed for 12 minutes, until the bacon is browned, crisp, and cooked through and an instant-read meat thermometer inserted into the center of a breast registers

75℃/165°F. You may need to add 2 minutes in the air fryer if the temperature is at 70℃/160°F.

4. Use kitchen tongs to transfer the breasts to a wire rack. Split the rolls open lengthwise and set them cut side down in the basket. Air-fry for 1 minute, or until warmed through.

5. Use kitchen tongs to transfer the rolls to a cutting board. Spread 1 tablespoon mayonnaise on the cut side of one half of each roll. Top with a chicken breast, lettuce leaf, and tomato slice. Serve warm.

6. **Variations & Ingredients Tips**:

7. Use turkey bacon for a lower-fat option.

8. Add sliced avocado or pickled onions for extra flavor and texture.

9. Toast the rolls before assembling the sandwiches for a crispy texture.

10. **Per Serving**: Calories: 640; Cholesterol: 110mg; Total Fat: 34g; Saturated Fat: 9g; Sodium: 1180mg; Total Carbohydrates: 44g; Dietary Fiber: 2g; Total Sugars: 5g; Protein: 42g

Chicken Gyros

Servings: 4
Prep Time: 10 Minutes (plus Marinating Time) | Cooking Time: 14 Minutes
Ingredients:

- 4 110to 140-gram boneless skinless chicken thighs, trimmed of any fat blobs
- 2 tablespoons Lemon juice
- 2 tablespoons Red wine vinegar
- 2 tablespoons Olive oil
- 2 teaspoons Dried oregano
- 2 teaspoons Minced garlic
- 1 teaspoon Table salt
- 1 teaspoon Ground black pepper
- 4 Pita pockets (gluten-free, if a concern)
- ½ cup Chopped tomatoes
- ½ cup Bottled regular, low-fat, or fat-free ranch dressing (gluten-free, if a concern)

Directions:

1. Mix the thighs, lemon juice, vinegar, oil, oregano, garlic, salt, and pepper in a zip-closed bag. Seal, gently massage the marinade into the meat through the plastic, and refrigerate for at least 2 hours or up to 6 hours. (Longer than that and the meat can turn rubbery.)

2. Set the plastic bag out on the counter (to make the contents a little less frigid). Preheat the air fryer to 190℃/375°F.

3. When the machine is at temperature, use kitchen tongs to place the thighs in the basket in one layer. Discard the marinade. Air-fry the chicken thighs undisturbed for 12 minutes, or until browned and an instant-read meat thermometer inserted into the thickest part of one thigh registers 75℃/165°F. You may need to air-fry the chicken 2 minutes longer if the machine's temperature is 70℃/360°F.

4. Use kitchen tongs to transfer the thighs to a cutting board. Cool for 5 minutes, then set one thigh in each of the pita pockets. Top each with 2 tablespoons chopped tomatoes and 2 tablespoons dressing. Serve warm.

5. **Variations & Ingredients Tips**:

6. Substitute chicken thighs with chicken breast for a leaner option.

7. Add shredded lettuce, sliced onions, or cucumbers for extra crunch and flavor.

8. Use homemade tzatziki sauce instead of ranch dressing for a more authentic taste.

9. **Per Serving**: Calories: 460; Cholesterol: 95mg; Total Fat: 28g; Saturated Fat: 5g; Sodium: 1070mg; Total Carbohydrates: 29g; Dietary Fiber: 2g; Total Sugars: 4g; Protein: 25g

Chicken Spiedies

Servings: 3
Prep Time: 15 Minutes (plus Marinating Time) | Cooking Time: 12 Minutes

Ingredients:

- 570 grams Boneless skinless chicken thighs, trimmed of any fat blobs and cut into 5-cm pieces
- 3 tablespoons Red wine vinegar
- 2 tablespoons Olive oil
- 2 tablespoons Minced fresh mint leaves
- 2 tablespoons Minced fresh parsley leaves
- 2 teaspoons Minced fresh dill fronds
- ¾ teaspoon Fennel seeds
- ¾ teaspoon Table salt
- Up to a ¼ teaspoon Red pepper flakes
- 3 Long soft rolls, such as hero, hoagie, or Italian sub rolls (gluten-free, if a concern), split open lengthwise
- 4½ tablespoons Regular or low-fat mayonnaise (not fat-free; gluten-free, if a concern)
- 1½ tablespoons Distilled white vinegar
- 1½ teaspoons Ground black pepper

Directions:

1. Mix the chicken, vinegar, oil, mint, parsley, dill, fennel seeds, salt, and red pepper flakes in a zip-closed plastic bag. Seal, gently massage the marinade ingredients into the meat, and refrigerate for at least 2 hours or up to 6 hours. (Longer than that and the meat can turn rubbery.)

2. Set the plastic bag out on the counter (to make the contents a little less frigid). Preheat the air fryer to 200℃/400°F.

3. When the machine is at temperature, use kitchen tongs to set the chicken thighs in the basket (discard any remaining marinade) and air-fry undisturbed for 6 minutes. Turn the thighs over and continue air-frying undisturbed for 6 minutes more, until well browned, cooked through, and even a little crunchy.

4. Dump the contents of the basket onto a wire rack and cool for 2 or 3 minutes. Divide the chicken evenly between the rolls. Whisk the mayonnaise, vinegar, and black pepper in a small bowl until smooth. Drizzle this sauce over the chicken pieces in the rolls.

5. **Variations & Ingredients Tips**:

6. Use chicken breast instead of thighs for a leaner option.

7. Substitute the herbs with your favorite combination, such as basil, oregano, or thyme.

8. Add sliced onions or pickled vegetables for extra crunch and tanginess.

9. **Per Serving**: Calories: 710; Cholesterol: 200mg; Total Fat: 44g; Saturated Fat: 8g; Sodium: 1240mg; Total Carbohydrates: 37g; Dietary Fiber: 2g; Total Sugars: 4g; Protein: 45g

Asian Glazed Meatballs

Servings: 4
Prep Time: 15 Minutes | Cooking Time: 10 Minutes

Ingredients:

- 1 large shallot, finely chopped
- 2 cloves garlic, minced
- 1 tablespoon grated fresh ginger
- 2 teaspoons fresh thyme, finely chopped
- 1½ cups brown mushrooms, very finely chopped (a food processor works well here)
- 2 tablespoons soy sauce
- freshly ground black pepper
- ½ kg ground beef

- ¼ kg ground pork
- 3 egg yolks
- 1 cup Thai sweet chili sauce (spring roll sauce)
- ¼ cup toasted sesame seeds
- 2 scallions, sliced

Directions:

1. Combine the shallot, garlic, ginger, thyme, mushrooms, soy sauce, freshly ground black pepper, ground beef and pork, and egg yolks in a bowl and mix the ingredients together. Gently shape the mixture into 24 balls, about the size of a golf ball.

2. Preheat the air fryer to 190℃/380°F.

3. Working in batches, air-fry the meatballs for 8 minutes, turning the meatballs over halfway through the cooking time. Drizzle some of the Thai sweet chili sauce on top of each meatball and return the basket to the air fryer, air-frying for another 2 minutes. Reserve the remaining Thai sweet chili sauce for serving.

4. As soon as the meatballs are done, sprinkle with toasted sesame seeds and transfer them to a serving platter. Scatter the scallions around and serve warm.

5. Variation and Ingredient Tips:

6. Use a food processor to finely chop the mushrooms for better texture in the meatballs.

7. Work in batches when air frying the meatballs to ensure even cooking and browning.

8. Drizzle the Thai sweet chili sauce over the meatballs towards the end of cooking for a nice glaze.

9. **Per Serving**: Calories: 550; Cholesterol: 205mg; Total Fat: 32g; Saturated Fat: 11g; Sodium: 1300mg; Total Carbohydrates: 36g; Dietary Fiber: 2g; Total Sugars: 23g; Protein: 29g

Provolone Stuffed Meatballs

Servings: 4
Prep Time: 20 Minutes | Cooking Time: 12 Minutes
Ingredients:

- 1 tablespoon olive oil
- 1 small onion, very finely chopped
- 1 to 2 cloves garlic, minced
- 340 grams ground beef
- 340 grams ground pork
- ¾ cup breadcrumbs
- ¼ cup grated Parmesan cheese
- ¼ cup finely chopped fresh parsley (or 1 tablespoon dried parsley)
- ½ teaspoon dried oregano

- 1½ teaspoons salt
- freshly ground black pepper
- 2 eggs, lightly beaten
- 140 grams sharp or aged provolone cheese, cut into 2.5-cm cubes

Directions:

1. Preheat a skillet over medium-high heat. Add the oil and cook the onion and garlic until tender, but not browned.

2. Transfer the onion and garlic to a large bowl and add the beef, pork, breadcrumbs, Parmesan cheese, parsley, oregano, salt, pepper and eggs. Mix well until all the ingredients are combined. Divide the mixture into 12 evenly sized balls. Make one meatball at a time, by pressing a hole in the meatball mixture with your finger and pushing a piece of provolone cheese into the hole. Mold the meat back into a ball, enclosing the cheese.

3. Preheat the air fryer to 190℃/380°F.

4. Working in two batches, transfer six of the meatballs to the air fryer basket and air-fry for 12 minutes, shaking the basket and turning the meatballs a couple of times during the cooking process. Repeat with the remaining six meatballs. You can pop the first batch of meatballs into the air fryer for the last two minutes of cooking to re-heat them. Serve warm.

5. **Variations & Ingredients Tips**:

6. Substitute beef and pork with ground turkey or chicken for a leaner meatball option.

7. Use mozzarella or fontina cheese instead of provolone for a milder flavor.

8. Serve meatballs with marinara sauce, in sub rolls, or over pasta for a complete meal.

9. **Per Serving** (3 meatballs): Calories: 520; Cholesterol: 180mg; Total Fat: 36g; Saturated Fat: 15g; Sodium: 1160mg; Total Carbohydrates: 18g; Dietary Fiber: 1g; Total Sugars: 2g; Protein: 35g

Inside-out Cheeseburgers

Servings: 3
Prep Time: 15 Minutes | Cooking Time: 9-11 Minutes
Ingredients:

- 510 grams 90% lean ground beef
- ¾ teaspoon Dried oregano
- ¾ teaspoon Table salt
- ¾ teaspoon Ground black pepper
- ¼ teaspoon Garlic powder

- 6 tablespoons (about 45 grams) Shredded Cheddar, Swiss, or other semi-firm cheese, or a purchased blend of shredded cheeses
- 3 Hamburger buns (gluten-free, if a concern), split open

Directions:

1. Preheat the air fryer to 190℃/375°F.
2. Gently mix the ground beef, oregano, salt, pepper, and garlic powder in a bowl until well combined without turning the mixture to mush. Form it into two 15-cm patties for the small batch, three for the medium, or four for the large.
3. Place 2 tablespoons of the shredded cheese in the center of each patty. With clean hands, fold the sides of the patty up to cover the cheese, then pick it up and roll it gently into a ball to seal the cheese inside. Gently press it back into a 12.5-cm burger without letting any cheese squish out. Continue filling and preparing more burgers, as needed.
4. Place the burgers in the basket in one layer and air-fry undisturbed for 8 minutes for medium or 10 minutes for well-done. (An instant-read meat thermometer won't work for these burgers because it will hit the mostly melted cheese inside and offer a hotter temperature than the surrounding meat.)
5. Use a nonstick-safe spatula, and perhaps a flatware fork for balance, to transfer the burgers to a cutting board. Set the buns cut side down in the basket in one layer (working in batches as necessary) and air-fry undisturbed for 1 minute, to toast a bit and warm up. Cool the burgers a few minutes more, then serve them warm in the buns.
6. **Variations & Ingredients Tips:**
7. Mix different types of cheese like cheddar, mozzarella, and blue cheese for a flavorful combination.
8. Add finely chopped bacon or caramelized onions to the cheese stuffing for extra richness.
9. Serve with your favorite burger toppings like lettuce, tomato, onion, and pickles.
10. **Per Serving** (1 burger): Calories: 480; Cholesterol: 125mg; Total Fat: 27g; Saturated Fat: 11g; Sodium: 720mg; Total Carbohydrates: 22g; Dietary Fiber: 1g; Total Sugars: 3g; Protein: 38g

- 510 grams Ground lamb
- 3 tablespoons Crumbled feta
- 1 teaspoon Minced garlic
- 1 teaspoon Tomato paste
- ¾ teaspoon Ground coriander
- ¾ teaspoon Ground dried ginger
- Up to ⅛ teaspoon Cayenne
- Up to a ⅛ teaspoon Table salt (optional)
- 3 Kaiser rolls or hamburger buns (gluten-free, if a concern), split open

Directions:

1. Preheat the air fryer to 190℃/375°F.
2. Gently mix the ground lamb, feta, garlic, tomato paste, coriander, ginger, cayenne, and salt (if using) in a bowl until well combined, trying to keep the bits of cheese intact. Form this mixture into two 15-cm patties for the small batch, three 12.5-cm patties for the medium, or four 12.5-cm patties for the large.
3. Set the patties in the basket in one layer and air-fry undisturbed for 16 minutes, or until an instant-read meat thermometer inserted into one burger registers 70℃/160°F. (The cheese is not an issue with the temperature probe in this recipe as it was for the Inside-Out Cheeseburgers, because the feta is so well mixed into the ground meat.)
4. Use a nonstick-safe spatula, and perhaps a flatware fork for balance, to transfer the burgers to a cutting board. Set the buns cut side down in the basket in one layer (working in batches as necessary) and air-fry undisturbed for 1 minute, to toast a bit and warm up. Serve the burgers warm in the buns.
5. **Variations & Ingredients Tips:**
6. Substitute feta with goat cheese or crumbled blue cheese for a different flavor profile.
7. Add finely chopped mint or parsley to the lamb mixture for a fresh, herbal taste.
8. Serve with tzatziki sauce, sliced cucumbers, and red onions for a Greek-inspired burger.
9. **Per Serving** (1 burger): Calories: 560; Cholesterol: 140mg; Total Fat: 34g; Saturated Fat: 15g; Sodium: 580mg; Total Carbohydrates: 25g; Dietary Fiber: 1g; Total Sugars: 3g; Protein: 38g

Lamb Burgers

Servings: 3
Prep Time: 15 Minutes | Cooking Time: 17 Minutes
Ingredients:

Dijon Thyme Burgers

Servings: 3
Prep Time: 15 Minutes | Cooking Time: 18 Minutes

Ingredients:

- 450 grams lean ground beef
- ⅓ cup panko breadcrumbs
- ¼ cup finely chopped onion
- 3 tablespoons Dijon mustard
- 1 tablespoon chopped fresh thyme
- 4 teaspoons Worcestershire sauce
- 1 teaspoon salt
- freshly ground black pepper
- Topping (optional):
- 2 tablespoons Dijon mustard
- 1 tablespoon dark brown sugar
- 1 teaspoon Worcestershire sauce
- 115 grams sliced Swiss cheese, optional

Directions:

1. Combine all the burger ingredients together in a large bowl and mix well. Divide the meat into 4 equal portions and then form the burgers, being careful not to over-handle the meat. One good way to do this is to throw the meat back and forth from one hand to another, packing the meat each time you catch it. Flatten the balls into patties, making an indentation in the center of each patty with your thumb (this will help it stay flat as it cooks) and flattening the sides of the burgers so that they will fit nicely into the air fryer basket.

2. Preheat the air fryer to 190℃/370°F.

3. If you don't have room for all four burgers, air-fry two or three burgers at a time for 8 minutes. Flip the burgers over and air-fry for another 6 minutes.

4. While the burgers are cooking combine the Dijon mustard, dark brown sugar, and Worcestershire sauce in a small bowl and mix well. This optional topping to the burgers really adds a boost of flavor at the end. Spread the Dijon topping evenly on each burger. If you cooked the burgers in batches, return the first batch to the cooker at this time – it's ok to place the fourth burger on top of the others in the center of the basket. Air-fry the burgers for another 3 minutes.

5. Finally, if desired, top each burger with a slice of Swiss cheese. Lower the air fryer temperature to 165℃/330°F and air-fry for another minute to melt the cheese. Serve the burgers on toasted brioche buns, dressed the way you like them.

6. **Variations & Ingredients Tips**:

7. Use ground turkey or chicken for a leaner burger option.

8. Add minced garlic or finely chopped herbs like parsley or chives for extra flavor.

9. Substitute panko breadcrumbs with regular breadcrumbs or oats for a different texture.

10. **Per Serving** (1 burger with cheese): Calories: 500; Cholesterol: 120mg; Total Fat: 27g; Saturated Fat: 11g; Sodium: 1180mg; Total Carbohydrates: 21g; Dietary Fiber: 1g; Total Sugars: 5g; Protein: 41g

Desserts And Sweets

Famous Chocolate Lava Cake

Servings: 4
Prep Time: 10 Minutes | Cooking Time: 15 Minutes

Ingredients:

- ¼ cup flour
- 1 tbsp cocoa powder
- ⅛ tsp salt
- ½ tsp baking powder
- 1 tsp vanilla extract
- ¼ cup raw honey
- 1 egg, beaten
- 2 tbsp olive oil
- 2 tbsp icing sugar, to dust

Directions:

1. Preheat air fryer to 190°C/380°F.
2. Sift the flour, cocoa powder, salt, vanilla, and baking powder in a bowl.
3. Add in honey, egg, and olive oil and stir to combine.
4. Divide the batter evenly among greased ramekins.
5. Put the filled ramekins inside the air fryer and Bake for 10 minutes.
6. Remove the lava cakes from the fryer and slide a knife around the outside edge of each cake.
7. Turn each ramekin upside down on a saucer and serve dusted with icing sugar.
8. **Variations & Ingredients Tips**:
9. Add a tablespoon of instant coffee or espresso powder to the batter for a mocha flavor.
10. Top with fresh berries, whipped cream, or a scoop of vanilla ice cream.
11. Use dark chocolate chunks instead of cocoa powder for a richer taste.
12. **Per Serving**: Calories: 250; Total Fat: 12g; Saturated Fat: 2g; Sodium: 230mg; Total Carbohydrates: 34g; Dietary Fiber: 1g; Total Sugars: 26g; Protein: 4g

Rich Blueberry Biscuit Shortcakes

Servings: 4
Prep Time: 20 Minutes | Cooking Time: 35 Minutes

Ingredients:

- 450-g blueberries, halved
- 1/4 cup granulated sugar
- 1 tsp orange zest
- 1 cup heavy cream
- 1 tbsp orange juice
- 2 tbsp powdered sugar
- 1/4 tsp cinnamon
- 1/4 tsp nutmeg
- 2 cups flour
- 1 egg yolk
- 1 tbsp baking powder
- 1/2 tsp baking soda
- 1/2 tsp cornstarch
- 1/2 tsp salt
- 1/2 tsp vanilla extract
- 1/2 tsp honey
- 4 tbsp cold butter, cubed
- 1 1/4 cups buttermilk

Directions:

1. Combine blueberries, granulated sugar, and orange zest in a bowl. Let chill the topping covered in the fridge until ready to use.
2. Beat heavy cream, orange juice, egg yolk, vanilla extract and powdered sugar in a metal bowl until peaks form. Let chill the whipped cream covered in the fridge until ready to use.
3. Preheat air fryer at 175°C/350°F.
4. Combine flour, cinnamon, nutmeg, baking powder, baking soda, cornstarch, honey, butter cubes, and buttermilk in a bowl until a sticky dough forms.
5. Flour your hands and form dough into 8 balls. Place them on a lightly greased pizza pan. Place pizza pan in the frying basket and Air Fry for 8 minutes.
6. Transfer biscuits to serving plates and cut them in half. Spread blueberry mixture to each biscuit bottom and place tops of biscuits. Garnish with whipped cream and serve.
7. **Variations & Ingredients Tips**:
8. Use other berries like raspberries or strawberries instead of blueberries.
9. Add lemon or lime zest to the whipped cream for extra flavor.

10. Brush the biscuit tops with melted butter before baking.

11. **Per serving**: Calories: 580; Total Fat: 33g; Saturated Fat: 20g; Cholesterol: 135mg; Sodium: 720mg; Total Carbs: 62g; Dietary Fiber: 2g; Total Sugars: 18g; Protein: 9g

Puff Pastry Apples

Servings: 4
Prep Time: 20 Minutes | Cooking Time: 10 Minutes
Ingredients:

- 3 Rome or Gala apples, peeled
- 2 tablespoons sugar
- 1 teaspoon all-purpose flour
- 1 teaspoon ground cinnamon
- 1/8 teaspoon ground ginger
- pinch ground nutmeg
- 1 sheet puff pastry
- 1 tablespoon butter, cut into 4 pieces
- 1 egg, beaten
- vegetable oil
- vanilla ice cream (optional)
- caramel sauce (optional)

Directions:

1. Remove the core from the apple by cutting the four sides off the apple around the core. Slice the pieces of apple into thin half-moons, about 6mm thick.

2. Combine the sugar, flour, cinnamon, ginger, and nutmeg in a large bowl. Add the apples to the bowl and gently toss until the apples are evenly coated with the spice mixture. Set aside.

3. Cut the puff pastry sheet into a 30cm by 30cm square. Then quarter the sheet into four 15cm squares. Save any remaining pastry for decorating the apples at the end.

4. Divide the spiced apples between the four puff pastry squares, stacking the apples in the center of each square and placing them flat on top of each other in a circle. Top the apples with a piece of the butter.

5. Brush the four edges of the pastry with the egg wash. Bring the four corners of the pastry together, wrapping them around the apple slices and pinching them together at the top in the style of a "beggars purse" appetizer. Fold the ends of the pastry corners down onto the apple making them look like leaves. Brush the entire apple with the egg wash.

6. Using the leftover dough, make leaves to decorate the apples. Cut out 8 leaf shapes, about 4cm long, "drawing" the leaf veins on the pastry leaves with a paring knife. Place 2 leaves on the top of each apple, tucking the ends of the leaves under the pastry in the center of the apples. Brush the top of the leaves with additional egg wash. Sprinkle the entire apple with some granulated sugar.

7. Preheat the air fryer to 175°C/350°F.

8. Spray or brush the inside of the air fryer basket with oil. Place the apples in the basket and air-fry for 6 minutes. Carefully turn the apples over – it's easiest to remove one apple, then flip the others over and finally return the last apple to the air fryer. Air-fry for an additional 4 minutes.

9. Serve the puff pastry apples warm with vanilla ice cream and drizzle with some caramel sauce.

10. **Variations & Ingredients Tips**:

11. Use different spices like allspice or cloves in the apple filling.

12. Brush the pastry with an egg wash before baking for a shiny finish.

13. Serve with whipped cream or powdered sugar instead of ice cream.

14. **Per serving**: Calories: 375; Total Fat: 20g; Saturated Fat: 6g; Cholesterol: 60mg; Sodium: 210mg; Total Carbs: 47g; Dietary Fiber: 3g; Total Sugars: 18g; Protein: 5g

Peanut Butter S'mores

Servings: 10
Prep Time: 10 Minutes | Cooking Time: 1 Minute
Ingredients:

- 10 Graham crackers (full, double-square cookies as they come out of the package)
- 5 tablespoons natural-style creamy or crunchy peanut butter
- 1/2 cup milk chocolate chips
- 10 standard-size marshmallows (not minis and not jumbo campfire ones)

Directions:

1. Preheat the air fryer to 175°C/350°F.

2. Break the graham crackers in half widthwise at the marked place, so the rectangle is now in two squares. Set half of the squares flat side up on your work surface. Spread each with about 1 1/2 teaspoons peanut butter, then set 10 to 12 chocolate chips point side up into the

peanut butter on each, pressing gently so the chips stick.

3. Flatten a marshmallow between your clean, dry hands and set it atop the chips. Do the same with the remaining marshmallows on the other coated graham crackers. Do not set the other half of the graham crackers on top of these coated graham crackers.

4. When the machine is at temperature, set the treats graham cracker side down in a single layer in the basket. They may touch, but even a fraction of an cm between them will provide better air flow. Air-fry undisturbed for 45 seconds.

5. Use a nonstick-safe spatula to transfer the topped graham crackers to a wire rack. Set the other graham cracker squares flat side down over the marshmallows. Cool for a couple of minutes before serving.

6. **Variations & Ingredients Tips**:

7. Substitute peanut butter with almond butter, cashew butter or Nutella.

8. Use dark chocolate chips or a mix of milk and dark for a richer flavor.

9. Sprinkle a pinch of sea salt on top of the peanut butter for a sweet and salty twist.

10. **Per serving**: Calories: 150; Total Fat: 7g; Saturated Fat: 2g; Cholesterol: 0mg; Sodium: 115mg; Total Carbs: 20g; Dietary Fiber: 1g; Total Sugars: 11g; Protein: 3g

Peach Cobbler

Servings: 4
Prep Time: 15 Minutes | Cooking Time: 12 Minutes
Ingredients:

* 450g frozen peaches, thawed, with juice (do not drain)
* 6 tablespoons sugar
* 1 tablespoon cornstarch
* 1 tablespoon water
* Crust:
* 1/2 cup flour
* 1/4 teaspoon salt
* 3 tablespoons butter
* 1 1/2 tablespoons cold water
* 1/4 teaspoon sugar

Directions:

1. Place peaches, including juice, and sugar in air fryer baking pan. Stir to mix well.

2. In a small cup, dissolve cornstarch in the water. Stir into peaches.

3. In a medium bowl, combine the flour and salt. Cut in butter using knives or a pastry blender. Stir in the cold water to make a stiff dough.

4. On a floured board or wax paper, pat dough into a square or circle slightly smaller than your air fryer baking pan. Cut diagonally into 4 pieces.

5. Place dough pieces on top of peaches, leaving a tiny bit of space between the edges. Sprinkle very lightly with sugar, no more than about 1/4 teaspoon.

6. Cook at 180°C/360°F for 12 minutes, until fruit bubbles and crust browns.

7. **Variations & Ingredients Tips**:

8. Use fresh peaches when in season for even better flavor.

9. Sprinkle cinnamon or nutmeg over the peaches before adding the crust.

10. Serve warm with a scoop of vanilla ice cream or dollop of whipped cream.

11. **Per serving**: Calories: 270; Total Fat: 9g; Saturated Fat: 6g; Cholesterol: 25mg; Sodium: 180mg; Total Carbs: 46g; Dietary Fiber: 2g; Total Sugars: 29g; Protein: 2g

Gingerbread

Servings: 6
Prep Time: 10 Minutes | Cooking Time: 20 Minutes
Ingredients:

* cooking spray
* 1 cup flour
* 2 tablespoons sugar
* ¾ teaspoon ground ginger
* ¼ teaspoon cinnamon
* 1 teaspoon baking powder
* ½ teaspoon baking soda
* ⅛ teaspoon salt
* 1 egg
* ¼ cup molasses
* ½ cup buttermilk
* 2 tablespoons oil
* 1 teaspoon pure vanilla extract

Directions:

1. Preheat air fryer to 165°C/330°F.

2. Spray 15x15-cm baking dish lightly with cooking spray.

3. In a medium bowl, mix together all the dry ingredients.

4. In a separate bowl, beat the egg. Add molasses, buttermilk, oil, and vanilla and stir until well mixed.

5. Pour liquid mixture into dry ingredients and stir until well blended.

6. Pour batter into baking dish and cook at 165°C/330°F for 20 minutes or until toothpick inserted in center of loaf comes out clean.

7. **Variations & Ingredients Tips**:

8. Add chopped candied ginger or crystallized ginger to the batter for extra spice.

9. Serve with a dollop of whipped cream or a scoop of vanilla ice cream.

10. Drizzle with lemon glaze or dust with powdered sugar before serving.

11. **Per Serving**: Calories: 220; Total Fat: 7g; Saturated Fat: 1g; Sodium: 270mg; Total Carbohydrates: 36g; Dietary Fiber: 1g; Total Sugars: 16g; Protein: 4g

Homemade Chips Ahoy

Servings: 4
Prep Time: 10 Minutes | Cooking Time: 20 Minutes
Ingredients:

- 1 tbsp coconut oil, melted
- 1 tbsp honey
- 1 tbsp milk
- 1/2 tsp vanilla extract
- 1/4 cup oat flour
- 2 tbsp coconut sugar
- 1/4 tsp salt
- 1/4 tsp baking powder
- 2 tbsp chocolate chips

Directions:

1. Combine coconut oil, honey, milk and vanilla in a bowl.

2. Add oat flour, coconut sugar, salt and baking powder. Stir until combined.

3. Fold in chocolate chips.

4. Preheat air fryer to 175°C/350°F.

5. Pour batter into a greased baking pan, leaving some space between portions.

6. Bake for 7 minutes until golden brown. Do not overbake.

7. Transfer to a cooling rack and serve chilled.

8. **Variations & Ingredients Tips**:

9. Use dairy-free milk and vegan chocolate chips for a vegan version.

10. Add chopped nuts or dried fruit to the batter.

11. Replace coconut sugar with brown sugar or maple syrup.

12. **Per Serving** (3 cookies): Calories: 148; Total Fat: 6g; Saturated Fat: 4g; Sodium: 116mg; Total Carbohydrates: 21g; Dietary Fiber: 2g; Total Sugars: 9g; Protein: 2g

Cheese & Honey Stuffed Figs

Servings: 4
Prep Time: 10 Minutes | Cooking Time: 15 Minutes
Ingredients:

- 8 figs, stem off
- 57 grams cottage cheese
- ¼ tsp ground cinnamon
- ¼ tsp orange zest
- ¼ tsp vanilla extract
- 2 tbsp honey
- 1 tbsp olive oil

Directions:

1. Preheat air fryer to 180°C/360°F.

2. Cut an "X" in the top of each fig 1/3 way through, leaving intact the base.

3. Mix together the cottage cheese, cinnamon, orange zest, vanilla extract and 1 tbsp of honey in a bowl.

4. Spoon the cheese mixture into the cavity of each fig.

5. Put the figs in a single layer in the air fryer basket. Drizzle the olive oil over the top of the figs and Roast for 10 minutes.

6. Drizzle with the remaining honey. Serve and enjoy!

7. **Variations & Ingredients Tips**:

8. Use ricotta, mascarpone, or goat cheese instead of cottage cheese.

9. Substitute figs with pitted dates or apricots.

10. Sprinkle with chopped pistachios or walnuts before serving.

11. **Per Serving**: Calories: 180; Total Fat: 6g; Saturated Fat: 1.5g; Sodium: 85mg; Total Carbohydrates: 30g; Dietary Fiber: 3g; Total Sugars: 26g; Protein: 4g

Caramel Apple Crumble

Servings: 6
Prep Time: 15 Minutes | Cooking Time: 50 Minutes

Ingredients:
- 4 apples, peeled and thinly sliced
- 2 tablespoons sugar
- 1 tablespoon flour
- 1 teaspoon ground cinnamon
- 1/4 teaspoon ground allspice
- Healthy pinch ground nutmeg
- 10 caramel squares, cut into small pieces
- Crumble Topping:
- 3/4 cup rolled oats
- 1/4 cup sugar
- 1/3 cup flour
- 1/4 teaspoon ground cinnamon
- 6 tablespoons butter, melted

Directions:
1. Preheat air fryer to 165°C/330°F.
2. Toss apples with sugar, flour, cinnamon, allspice, nutmeg and caramel pieces.
3. Pour into a 15cm baking dish.
4. Make topping by mixing oats, sugar, flour, cinnamon and melted butter.
5. Top apples with crumble mixture. Cover dish with foil.
6. Air fry for 25 mins, then remove foil and cook 25 more mins.
7. Serve warm, with ice cream or whipped cream if desired.
8. **Variations & Ingredients Tips:**
9. Use a mixture of baking apples like Honeycrisp and Granny Smith.
10. Add chopped pecans or walnuts to the crumble topping.
11. Drizzle with extra caramel sauce before serving.
12. **Per Serving:** Calories: 365; Total Fat: 14g; Saturated Fat: 7g; Sodium: 86mg; Total Carbohydrates: 60g; Dietary Fiber: 4g; Total Sugars: 35g; Protein: 3g

Thumbprint Sugar Cookies

Servings: 10
Prep Time: 15 Minutes | Cooking Time: 8 Minutes
Ingredients:
- 2 1/2 tablespoons butter
- 1/3 cup cane sugar
- 1 teaspoon pure vanilla extract
- 1 large egg
- 1 cup all-purpose flour

- 1/2 teaspoon baking soda
- 1/4 teaspoon salt
- 10 chocolate kisses

Directions:
1. Preheat the air fryer to 175°C/350°F.
2. In a large bowl, cream the butter with the sugar and vanilla. Whisk in the egg and set aside.
3. In a separate bowl, mix the flour, baking soda, and salt. Then gently mix the dry ingredients into the wet.
4. Portion the dough into 10 balls; then press down on each with the bottom of a cup to create a flat cookie.
5. Liberally spray the metal trivet of an air fryer basket with olive oil mist.
6. Place the cookies in the air fryer basket on the trivet and cook for 8 minutes or until the tops begin to lightly brown.
7. Remove and immediately press the chocolate kisses into the tops of the cookies while still warm.
8. Let cool 5 minutes and then enjoy.
9. **Variations & Ingredients Tips:**
10. Roll dough balls in colored sanding sugar before baking.
11. Use different candy or nut toppings.
12. Make with a gluten-free flour blend.
13. **Per serving:** Calories: 150; Total Fat: 6g; Saturated Fat: 3g; Cholesterol: 25mg; Sodium: 160mg; Total Carbs: 22g; Dietary Fiber: 1g; Total Sugars: 10g; Protein: 2g

Mango-chocolate Custard

Servings: 4
Prep Time: 15 Minutes | Cooking Time: 40 Minutes
Ingredients:
- 4 egg yolks
- 2 tbsp granulated sugar
- 1/8 tsp almond extract
- 1 1/2 cups half-and-half
- 3/4 cup chocolate chips
- 1 mango, pureed
- 1 mango, chopped
- 1 tsp fresh mint, chopped

Directions:
1. Beat egg yolks, sugar and almond extract. Set aside.
2. Warm half-and-half in a saucepan until simmering.
3. Whisk some half-and-half into egg mixture, then whisk egg mixture into saucepan.

4. Stir in chocolate chips and mango puree for 10 mins until melted.

5. Divide custard into 4 ramekins.

6. Preheat air fryer to 175°C/350°F.

7. Bake ramekins for 6-8 minutes.

8. Cool, then chill in fridge for 2 hours up to 2 days.

9. Serve topped with chopped mango and mint.

10. **Variations & Ingredients Tips**:

11. Use coconut milk instead of half-and-half.

12. Add a splash of rum or orange liqueur.

13. Top with toasted coconut or crushed cookies.

14. **Per Serving**: Calories: 350; Total Fat: 21g; Saturated Fat: 11g; Sodium: 62mg; Total Carbohydrates: 35g; Dietary Fiber: 3g; Total Sugars: 27g; Protein: 7g

Dark Chokolate Cookies

Servings: 4
Prep Time: 20 Minutes | Cooking Time: 50 Minutes
Ingredients:

- 1/3 cup brown sugar
- 2 tbsp butter, softened
- 1 egg yolk
- 2/3 cup flour
- 5 tbsp peanut butter
- ¼ tsp baking soda
- 1 tsp dark rum
- ½ cup dark chocolate chips

Directions:

1. Preheat air fryer to 155°C/310°F.

2. Beat butter and brown sugar in a bowl until fluffy. Stir in the egg yolk.

3. Add flour, 3 tbsp of peanut butter, baking soda, and rum until well mixed.

4. Spread the batter into a parchment-lined baking pan. Bake in the air fryer until the cooking is lightly brown and just set, 7-10 minutes.

5. Remove from the fryer and let cool for 10 minutes.

6. After, remove the cookie from the pan and the parchment paper and cool on the wire rack.

7. When cooled, combine the chips with the remaining peanut butter in a heatproof cup. Place in the air fryer and Bake until melted, 2 minutes. Remove and stir.

8. Spread on the cooled cookies and serve.

9. **Variations & Ingredients Tips**:

10. Use milk chocolate or white chocolate chips for a sweeter cookie.

11. Substitute dark rum with vanilla extract for an alcohol-free version.

12. Add chopped nuts like almonds or hazelnuts to the batter.

13. **Per Serving**: Calories: 430; Total Fat: 24g; Saturated Fat: 9g; Sodium: 260mg; Total Carbohydrates: 51g; Dietary Fiber: 3g; Total Sugars: 30g; Protein: 8g

Coconut Cream Roll-ups

Servings: 4
Prep Time: 15 Minutes | Cooking Time: 20 Minutes
Ingredients:

- 1/2 cup cream cheese, softened
- 1 cup fresh raspberries
- 1/4 cup brown sugar
- 1/4 cup coconut cream
- 1 egg
- 1 tsp corn starch
- 6 spring roll wrappers

Directions:

1. Preheat air fryer to 175°C/350°F.

2. Mix cream cheese, brown sugar, coconut cream, cornstarch and egg until fluffy.

3. Spoon filling onto spring roll wrappers and top with raspberries.

4. Roll up wrappers around filling and seal with water.

5. Place seam-side down on foil-lined air fryer basket.

6. Bake for 10 minutes, flipping once, until golden.

7. Remove with tongs and serve hot or cold.

8. **Variations & Ingredients Tips**:

9. Use other berries like blueberries or strawberries.

10. Add shredded coconut to the filling.

11. Drizzle with melted white or dark chocolate after baking.

12. **Per Serving**: Calories: 247; Total Fat: 13g; Saturated Fat: 8g; Sodium: 167mg; Total Carbohydrates: 28g; Dietary Fiber: 3g; Total Sugars: 15g; Protein: 5g

Berry Streusel Cake

Servings: 6
Prep Time: 15 Minutes | Cooking Time: 60 Minutes
Ingredients:

- 2 tbsp demerara sugar
- 2 tbsp sunflower oil
- 1/4 cup almond flour
- 1 cup pastry flour
- 1/2 cup brown sugar
- 1 tsp baking powder
- 1 tbsp lemon zest
- 1/4 tsp salt
- 3/4 cup milk
- 2 tbsp olive oil
- 1 tsp vanilla
- 1 cup blueberries
- 1/2 cup powdered sugar
- 1 tbsp lemon juice
- 1/8 tsp salt

Directions:

1. Mix demerara sugar, sunflower oil, and almond flour. Refrigerate.
2. Whisk pastry flour, brown sugar, baking powder, zest, and 1/4 tsp salt.
3. Add milk, olive oil, vanilla and stir until combined. Fold in blueberries.
4. Oil a baking pan and pour in batter.
5. Preheat air fryer to 155°C/310°F.
6. Top batter with chilled almond mixture.
7. Bake for 45 mins until a toothpick inserted comes out clean.
8. Make icing with powdered sugar, lemon juice and 1/8 tsp salt.
9. Let cake cool, slice into 6 pieces and drizzle with icing.
10. **Variations & Ingredients Tips**:
11. Use raspberries or strawberries instead of blueberries.
12. Add sliced almonds or pecans to the streusel topping.
13. Substitute buttermilk for regular milk.
14. **Per Serving**: Calories: 333; Total Fat: 13g; Saturated Fat: 2g; Sodium: 193mg; Total Carbohydrates: 50g; Dietary Fiber: 3g; Total Sugars: 27g; Protein: 5g

Fried Pineapple Chunks

Servings: 3
Prep Time: 20 Minutes | Cooking Time: 10 Minutes
Ingredients:

- 3 tablespoons Cornstarch
- 1 Large egg white, beaten until foamy
- 1 cup (113 grams) Ground vanilla wafer cookies (not low-fat cookies)
- ¼ teaspoon Ground dried ginger
- 18 (about 2¼ cups) Fresh 2.5-cm chunks peeled and cored pineapple

Directions:

1. Preheat the air fryer to 200°C/400°F.
2. Put the cornstarch in a medium or large bowl. Put the beaten egg white in a small bowl. Pour the cookie crumbs and ground dried ginger into a large zip-closed plastic bag, shaking it a bit to combine them.
3. Dump the pineapple chunks into the bowl with the cornstarch. Toss and stir until well coated. Use your cleaned fingers or a large fork like a shovel to pick up a few pineapple chunks, shake off any excess cornstarch, and put them in the bowl with the egg white. Stir gently, then pick them up and let any excess egg white slip back into the rest. Put them in the bag with the crumb mixture. Repeat the cornstarch-then-egg process until all the pineapple chunks are in the bag. Seal the bag and shake gently, turning the bag this way and that, to coat the pieces well.
4. Set the coated pineapple chunks in the basket with as much air space between them as possible. Even a fraction of 0.25 cm will work, but they should not touch. Air-fry undisturbed for 10 minutes, or until golden brown and crisp.
5. Gently dump the contents of the basket onto a wire rack. Cool for at least 5 minutes or up to 15 minutes before serving.
6. **Variations & Ingredients Tips**:
7. Substitute pineapple with mango, papaya, or apple chunks.
8. Use cinnamon, nutmeg, or cardamom instead of ginger for different spice flavors.
9. Serve with a scoop of coconut ice cream or a drizzle of rum caramel sauce.
10. **Per Serving**: Calories: 320; Total Fat: 12g; Saturated Fat: 3.5g; Sodium: 170mg; Total Carbohydrates: 50g; Dietary Fiber: 2g; Total Sugars: 30g; Protein: 4g

Sultana & Walnut Stuffed Apples

Servings: 4

Prep Time: 10 Minutes | Cooking Time: 30 Minutes

Ingredients:

- 4 apples, cored and halved
- 2 tablespoons lemon juice
- 1/4 cup sultana raisins
- 3 tablespoons chopped walnuts
- 3 tablespoons dried cranberries
- 2 tablespoons packed brown sugar
- 1/3 cup apple cider
- 1 tablespoon cinnamon

Directions:

1. Preheat air fryer to 175°C/350°F.
2. Spritz the apples with lemon juice and put them in a baking pan.
3. Combine the raisins, cinnamon, walnuts, cranberries, and brown sugar, then spoon 1/4 of the mix into the apples.
4. Drizzle the apple cider around the apples, Bake for 13-18 minutes until softened.
5. Serve warm.
6. **Variations & Ingredients Tips**:
7. Use other dried fruits like apricots, dates or prunes.
8. Add a pinch of nutmeg or allspice to the spice mix.
9. Drizzle with honey or maple syrup before serving.
10. **Per serving**: Calories: 230; Total Fat: 6g; Saturated Fat: 1g; Cholesterol: 0mg; Sodium: 15mg; Total Carbs: 45g; Dietary Fiber: 5g; Total Sugars: 35g; Protein: 3g

Cinnamon Pear Cheesecake

Servings: 6
Prep Time: 20 Minutes | Cooking Time: 60 Minutes + Cooling Time

Ingredients:

- 450-g cream cheese, softened
- 1 cup crumbled graham crackers
- 4 peeled pears, sliced
- 1 tsp vanilla extract
- 1 tbsp brown sugar
- 1 tsp ground cinnamon
- 1 egg
- 1 cup condensed milk
- 2 tbsp white sugar
- 1 1/2 tsp butter, melted

Directions:

1. Preheat air fryer to 175°C/350°F.
2. Mix graham cracker crumbs, white sugar and melted butter. Press into greased pan.
3. Bake crust for 5 minutes. Let cool 30 minutes to harden.
4. Beat cream cheese, vanilla, brown sugar, cinnamon, condensed milk and egg.
5. Arrange pear slices over crust and top with cream cheese mixture.
6. Bake for 40 minutes until set.
7. Allow to cool completely before serving.
8. **Variations & Ingredients Tips**:
9. Use gingersnaps or biscoff cookies for the crust.
10. Top with streusel or granola before baking.
11. Substitute apple slices or mixed berries for the pears.
12. **Per Serving**: Calories: 508; Total Fat: 26g; Saturated Fat: 14g; Sodium: 424mg; Total Carbohydrates: 58g; Dietary Fiber: 2g; Total Sugars: 40g; Protein: 11g

Donut Holes

Servings: 13
Prep Time: 15 Minutes | Cooking Time: 12 Minutes

Ingredients:

- 6 tablespoons Granulated white sugar
- 1½ tablespoons Butter, melted and cooled
- 2 tablespoons (or 1 small egg, well beaten) Pasteurized egg substitute, such as Egg Beaters
- 6 tablespoons Regular or low-fat sour cream (not fat-free)
- ¾ teaspoon Vanilla extract
- 1⅔ cups All-purpose flour
- ¾ teaspoon Baking powder
- ¼ teaspoon Table salt
- Vegetable oil spray

Directions:

1. Preheat the air fryer to 180°C/350°F.
2. Whisk the sugar and melted butter in a medium bowl until well combined. Whisk in the egg substitute or egg, then the sour cream and vanilla until smooth. Remove the whisk and stir in the flour, baking powder, and salt with a wooden spoon just until a soft dough forms.
3. Use 2 tablespoons of this dough to create a ball between your clean palms. Set it aside and continue

making balls: 8 more for the small batch, 12 more for the medium batch, or 17 more for the large one.

4. Coat the balls in the vegetable oil spray, then set them in the basket with as much air space between them as possible. Even a fraction of 0.25 cm will be enough, but they should not touch. Air-fry undisturbed for 12 minutes, or until browned and cooked through. A toothpick inserted into the center of a ball should come out clean.

5. Pour the contents of the basket onto a wire rack. Cool for at least 5 minutes before serving.

6. **Variations & Ingredients Tips**:

7. Toss the warm donut holes in cinnamon sugar or powdered sugar.

8. Add grated lemon or orange zest to the batter for a citrusy flavor.

9. Fill the donut holes with jam, Nutella, or pastry cream using a piping bag.

10. **Per Serving**: Calories: 130; Total Fat: 5g; Saturated Fat: 3g; Sodium: 100mg; Total Carbohydrates: 20g; Dietary Fiber: 0g; Total Sugars: 9g; Protein: 2g

Blueberry Crisp

Servings: 6
Prep Time: 10 Minutes | Cooking Time: 13 Minutes
Ingredients:
- 3 cups Fresh or thawed frozen blueberries
- 1/3 cup Granulated white sugar
- 1 tablespoon Instant tapioca
- 1/3 cup All-purpose flour
- 1/3 cup Rolled oats (not quick-cooking or steel-cut)
- 1/3 cup Chopped walnuts or pecans
- 1/3 cup Packed light brown sugar
- 5 tablespoons plus 1 teaspoon (2/3 stick) Butter, melted and cooled
- 3/4 teaspoon Ground cinnamon
- 1/4 teaspoon Table salt

Directions:
1. Preheat the air fryer to 200°C/400°F.
2. Mix the blueberries, granulated sugar, and instant tapioca in a 15cm, 18cm or 20cm round cake pan.
3. Set the pan in the basket and air-fry for 5 minutes, until blueberries begin to bubble.
4. Meanwhile, mix flour, oats, nuts, brown sugar, butter, cinnamon, and salt in a bowl.

5. When blueberries bubble, crumble flour mixture evenly on top.

6. Continue air-frying for 8 minutes until topping is browned and filling is bubbling.

7. Transfer pan to a wire rack and cool at least 10 minutes before serving.

8. **Variations & Ingredients Tips**:

9. Use other berries like raspberries or blackberries.

10. Add lemon or orange zest to the crisp topping.

11. Serve warm with a scoop of vanilla ice cream.

12. **Per Serving**: Calories: 322; Total Fat: 15g; Saturated Fat: 6g; Sodium: 122mg; Total Carbohydrates: 45g; Dietary Fiber: 3g; Total Sugars: 25g; Protein: 4g

Keto Cheesecake Cups

Servings: 6
Prep Time: 10 Minutes | Cooking Time: 10 Minutes
Ingredients:
- 225-g cream cheese
- 1/4 cup plain whole-milk Greek yogurt
- 1 large egg
- 1 teaspoon pure vanilla extract
- 3 tablespoons monk fruit sweetener
- 1/4 teaspoon salt
- 1/2 cup walnuts, roughly chopped

Directions:
1. Preheat the air fryer to 155°C/315°F.
2. Beat the cream cheese with yogurt, egg, vanilla, sweetener and salt until combined.
3. Fold in the chopped walnuts.
4. Fill 6 silicone muffin liners with the batter. Place in an air fryer pan.
5. Carefully put the pan in the air fryer basket and cook for 10 minutes until lightly browned.
6. Refrigerate the cheesecake cups for 3 hours before serving.
7. **Variations & Ingredients Tips**:
8. Use other keto-friendly sweeteners like erythritol or stevia.
9. Add lemon or orange zest to the batter.
10. Top with fresh berries or sugar-free chocolate syrup.
11. **Per Serving**: Calories: 205; Total Fat: 18g; Saturated Fat: 9g; Sodium: 166mg; Total Carbohydrates: 4g; Dietary Fiber: 1g; Total Sugars: 2g; Protein: 6g

INDEX

A

B

Buttery Lobster Tails 52

C

Cajun Chicken Livers 33

Cajun Flounder Fillets 48

Cajun Fried Chicken 28

Cajun Pork Loin Chops 40

Caramel Apple Crumble 86

Caribbean Jerk Cod Fillets 46

Carrot Orange Muffins 14

Cayenne-spiced Roasted Pecans 27

Charred Cauliflower Tacos 58

Cheddar-pimiento Strips 22

Cheese & Honey Stuffed Figs 86

Cheesy Chicken Tenders 31

Chicken Apple Brie Melt 75

Chicken Club Sandwiches 78

Chicken Gyros 78

Chicken Hand Pies 29

Chicken Salad With Roasted Vegetables 32

Chicken Salad With Sunny Citrus Dressing 64

Chicken Saltimbocca Sandwiches 76

Chicken Spiedies 79

Chili Cheese Dogs 72

Cinnamon Pear Cheesecake 90

Cinnamon Rolls With Cream Cheese Glaze 15

Coconut Cream Roll-ups 88

Coconut Mini Tarts 16

Corned Beef Hash 37

Country-style Pork Ribs(1) 40

Crab Stuffed Salmon Roast 50

Crab Toasts 25

Crispy Bacon 16

Crispy, Cheesy Leeks 65

Crunchy Falafel Balls 74

Crunchy Parmesan Edamame 23

Curried Cauliflower 57

D

Dark Chokolate Cookies 88

Dijon Thyme Burgers 82

Donut Holes 90

E

Effortless Mac `n´ Cheese 56

F

Falafel 60

Famous Chocolate Lava Cake 83

Fancy Chicken Piccata 30

Favorite Fried Chicken Wings 28

Fish Goujons With Tartar Sauce 48

Five-spice Roasted Sweet Potatoes 69

French Fries 66

French Toast Sticks Recipes 17

Fried Bananas 21

Fried Eggplant Slices 70

Fried Gyoza 23

Fried Pineapple Chunks 89

Fried Rice With Curried Tofu 55

G

Garlic-lemon Steamer Clams 51

General Tso's Cauliflower 71

German-style Pork Patties 40

Gingerbread 85

Green Strata 13

Ground Beef Calzones 39

H

Hasselbacks 68

Healthy Living Mushroom Enchiladas 59

Homemade Chips Ahoy 86

Home-style Fish Sticks 49

Home-style Taro Chips 24

Honey Pork Links 43

Honey-lemon Chicken Wings 27

Hot Cheese Bites 24

I

Indian Fry Bread Tacos 37

Inside-out Cheeseburgers 80

Italian Bruschetta With Mushrooms & Cheese 21

K

Kentucky-style Pork Tenderloin 41

Keto Cheesecake Cups 91

L

Lamb Burger With Feta And Olives 38

Parmesan Pizza Nuggets 20

Parsley Egg Scramble With Cottage Cheese 13

Peach Cobbler 85

Peachy Pork Chops 43

Peanut Butter S'mores 84

Peanut-crusted Salmon 47

Pecan-crusted Tilapia 54

Pecan-orange Crusted Striped Bass 50

Perfect Broccolini 67

Perfect Burgers 73

Philly Cheesesteak Sandwiches 74

Pinto Bean Casserole 58

Pizza Margherita With Spinach 63

Provolone Stuffed Meatballs 80

Puff Pastry Apples 84

Q

Quesadillas 18

R

Restaurant-style Chicken Thighs 28

Reuben Sandwiches 72

Rich Baked Sweet Potatoes 70

Rich Blueberry Biscuit Shortcakes 83

Roasted Herbed Shiitake Mushrooms 68

Roasted Vegetable Thai Green Curry 57

Roasted Vegetable, Brown Rice And Black Bean Burrito 58

S

Sausage And Pepper Heros 75

T

Traditional Moo Shu Pork Lettuce Wraps 43

Tuna Patties With Dill Sauce 52

Turkey & Rice Frittata 34

Turkey Burger Sliders 20

Tuscan Stuffed Chicken 30

U

Uncle's Potato Wedges 26

V

Vegetarian Stuffed Bell Peppers 55

Veggie-stuffed Bell Peppers 60

W

Walnut Pancake 13

White Bean Veggie Burgers 73

Y

Yogurt-marinated Chicken Legs 34

Z

Zucchini Walnut Bread 16

Printed in Great Britain
by Amazon